Advanced Business for Innovation

Stimulate Competitor Innovation and Copying

Donald Mitchell

Author of *Advanced Business,*
Business Basics, and *Excellent Solutions*
Coauthor of *The 2,000 Percent Solution* and
The 2,000 Percent Squared Solution

400 Year Project Press
Weston, Massachusetts
United States of America

Advanced Business for Innovation
Stimulate Competitor Innovation and Copying

ISBN: 978-0692439104
0692439102

For information, contact:

Donald W. Mitchell
400 Year Project Press
P.O. Box 302
Weston, Massachusetts 02493
781-647-4211

Published in the United States of America

This book is dedicated to:

Members of The Billionaire Entrepreneurs' Master Mind

May quickly and easily innovating and
encouraging helpful competitor innovation and copying
always be ahead of them!

And their spouses, their children and grandchildren,
and their descendants

May this book help them to always focus
on the Lord and doing His will!

Contents

Acknowledgments

Oh, give thanks to the LORD!
Call upon His name;
Make known His deeds among the peoples!

— 1 Chronicles 16:8 (NKJV)

I thank Almighty God, our Heavenly Father, for creating the universe and all the people on the Earth; our Lord and Savior, Jesus Christ, for providing the way for us to gain Salvation; and the Holy Spirit for guiding our daily paths towards repentance and righteousness. I also humbly acknowledge the perfect guidance I received from God through the Holy Spirit and His Word to write this book.

I feel deeply honored by Professor Wayne P. Jones, Ph.D., writing the book's excellent foreword. Professor Jones is someone I've enjoyed watching as he went from being a practitioner to an expert who informs many others so they can accomplish much more. He has captured the essence of *Advanced Business for Innovation* in a way that will enrich your understanding of the book's contents. I hope you will have a chance to meet and work with him.

I am grateful to Peter Drucker for encouraging me to write about 2,000 percent solutions (ways of accomplishing twenty times more with the same or less time, effort, and resources) and to seek ever-simpler ways to help people learn to employ them. His faith in this method for solving problems caused me to take much more seriously the opportunity to share what I had been doing.

I appreciate all those who have permitted me to share with them 2,000 percent solution methods and the work of The 400 Year Project in improving far beyond them. I thank those who have applied what they learned for all the insights I have gained from observing their wonderful work.

I once again thank Derrick Z. Jackson for supplying the delightful cover image that so beautifully encapsulates the book's key concept: attracting others to follow the same innovative pathways.

I can never thank my family enough for allowing me the time and peace to work on such a huge and awe-inspiring project for God. They made many sacrifices without complaining and have been a continual inspiration.

I appreciate my many clients who held off on their demands for my help so that this project could receive the attention it required. Their financial support also made it possible for me to give this time to the Lord and to invest in the expenses for making this book available.

Finally, I am most appreciative of the many fine improvements that my editor, Bernice Pettinato, made in the text. This is the seventeenth book where she has helped make the messages clearer and more pleasant to read. As always, she was a delight to work with. Her kindness made the writing much easier. I value all she has taught me about writing. I look forward to learning new lessons from her during future books.

I accept sole responsibility for any remaining errors and apologize to my readers for any difficulties and inconveniences that they encounter as a consequence.

Foreword

As a professor who has been teaching and consulting in innovation, entrepreneurship, and creativity for almost twenty years, I frequently look at new works in these areas. Several years ago, Don Mitchell reached out to me to review one of his earlier books. Though we had not seen each other in a number of years, I was glad he remembered me and pleased to help. More importantly, I enjoyed the book.

I first met Don Mitchell in the mid 1970s when he was a consultant with The Boston Consulting Group (BCG) and I was a young marketing director at Heublein, Inc. Heublein had hired BCG to facilitate a strategic-planning effort and had selected a group of promising young managers to work with BCG. I was lucky enough to be in that group. Over the next year or so I worked very closely with Don and learned what constituted good strategy making and planning. More importantly, I saw the depth of his character. Even at that young age, he demonstrated what has become his "purpose-driven life." Don has become a key voice that needs to be heard and understood by American business.

When Don asked me to write a foreword for *Advanced Business for Innovation*, I was honored. Seldom does one get the chance to make a contribution, albeit a small one, to a book that is destined to make a substantial contribution to the practice of management.

Advanced Business for Innovation: Stimulate Competitor Innovation and Copying is a thought-provoking work. The book's premise is that encouraging others to innovate is a powerful tool for increasing a company's own innovations. We all like to compete, and we need better competition to improve our own efforts. *Advanced Business for Innovation* is not just one book, but, rather, five books.

It is divided into four sections, and each section is sufficiently important to justify being a complete book. The fifth section is Don's personal testimony and provides powerful insight into understanding his work.

Part One describes many actions that a company can take that will increase industry innovation and serve as a stimulus to improve itself. Part Two shifts to increasing customer effectiveness in using innovative offerings. Part Three addresses powerful ways to encourage employees to make innovation breakthroughs. Part Four turns to the intriguing topic of actions to take in conjunction with competitors that will increase their innovation for the purpose of learning and feeling encouraged to do more innovation in one's own company.

The book can be used a number of ways. First, the entire book can be read as one usually reads a business book. Second, a reader could decide to tackle one section at a time. As I said, each section easily constitutes a comprehensive treatment of the topic.

Because each of the four sections is subdivided into a series of "lessons" and "lesson assignments" (fifty lessons and assignments in all), the book is ideal as a teaching/training vehicle. I can easily see a company adopting the book as a training aid where employees read and then meet to discuss the assignments in small groups.

As I reviewed the book, I thought back over thirty years to an early meeting with Don Mitchell. As part of the BCG process, Don asked me to prepare a document discussing what I saw as problems Heublein was facing. I sent the document to Don and we agreed to meet to discuss my work. A few days later, we met at a restaurant in Hartford, Connecticut. Don was gracious but tore my work apart! Without going into all the details, his key point was that I needed to think "longer, deeper, and harder" about what I was doing. That lesson stayed with me over the years, and I think it is partly the reason I have achieved some degree of success. *Advanced Business for Innovation* is much like that: It shows the reader how to think longer, deeper and harder about ways to improve the organization, an important lesson for most organizations.

As a practicing Christian, I fully appreciate Don's approach in this and his other books. However, I know that some readers can be put off by what they perceive as religiosity. Regardless of where you fall on the religious continuum, I urge you to read this book. This book sets the stage for exceptional performance and does so within the context of enduring religious principles. In my humble opinion, this is exactly what this world needs today. By writing this and other books, Don Mitchell has set the table for learning. Enjoy the feast!

Wayne P. Jones, Ph.D.
Executive in Residence
Professor of Marketing
College of Business
University of Louisville

Louisville, Kentucky
April 2015

Introduction

"You are the light of the world.
A city that is set on a hill cannot be hidden.

"Nor do they light a lamp and
put it under a basket,
but on a lampstand,
and it gives light
to all who are in the house."

— Matthew 5:14-15 (NKJV)

The information in *Advanced Business for Innovation: Stimulate Competitor Innovation and Copying* has been selected from among The 400 Year Project's most powerful, easily appreciated, and readily applicable lessons revealed during the project's 19 years of research and practice. Many of these lessons were initially developed during 2011 and 2012 for The Billionaire Entrepreneurs' Master Mind, a consortium of entrepreneurs learning and applying the latest generation of The 400 Year Project's best practices to achieve success beyond the usual kind of breakthroughs. Versions of seven lessons in *Advanced Business for Innovation* also appear in the for-profit edition of *Excellent Solutions* (400 Year Project Press, 2014). All the lessons have deep roots in earlier research and testing done by Outstanding Chief Executive Officers, a partnership of global leaders Carol Coles and I directed to develop many of the current best practices for accelerating innovation. All fifty lessons have been updated and improved to increase their usefulness.

Advanced Business for Innovation: Stimulate Competitor Innovation and Copying is different from many other innovation books in primarily paying attention to what a company can do to shape an industry to be more innovative, to make customers more effective, and to stimulate increased and faster innovation and copying by competitors, rather than on just what an organization should do in innovating. As such, this book provides a more holistic approach, seeking to develop more relevant aspects of an environment that increase helpful innovation. In taking this approach, however, I acknowledge that research on how individuals and groups become more innovative can be applied with what *Advanced Business for Innovation* discusses.

I believe that the words of Jesus in Matthew 5:14-15 (NKJV) capture this book's perspective very well. To paraphrase His wisdom in terms of this book's topic, I observe as follows: If you set a good example in innovating, that example will become the way those in your industry think and act.

I need a little extra help from you as we think together about encouraging innovation and copying by your competitors. For the first time in books by The 400 Year Project (documenting ways to accomplish improvements at least 20 times faster with the same or fewer resources, time, and effort — www.fastforward400.com) books, I am developing methods for a complementary 2,000 percent solution whose benefits may not be entirely clear to you as we begin.

In fact, your instincts and what you have read may have focused on just the opposite point of view: *Discourage* competitors from innovating and copying you.

Will you suspend your disbelief, please, for a few lessons? In that material, I develop the case for why this goal and related activities can add great value when applied in conjunction with the first four complementary breakthroughs (gaining market share while accelerating market growth by 20 times, reducing stakeholder and company costs of an offering by at least 96 percent, eliminating 96 percent of investment needed to supply offerings, and increasing value for all stakeholders by 20 times) that are discussed in *Business Basics* and *Advanced Business*.

Thank you. I appreciate your open-mindedness.

Let me begin by sharing what I have published previously on this subject. The following material is drawn from Chapter 11 of *Adventures of an Optimist* (Mitchell and Company Press, 2007) in which I lay out the case for the exponential benefit expansions that can follow from organizations combining several complementary breakthroughs (ways of enhancing results by at least 20 times with the same or fewer resources, time, and effort that fully multiply the benefits of one another):

> Isn't it great that people are such copy cats? This virtually universal instinct can be relied on to help us create another 20 times boost in benefits: an increase in the number of people who apply the same improvements as do the most successful creators of multiple 2,000 percent solutions.
>
> Many people will be aghast at the suggestion. Why make it easier for others to copy you? Isn't it better to keep your best methods a secret? Well, while that approach often works best, it's not always the case.
>
> In many instances, an industry is being held back by the unprofessional way that some competitors operate. Improve the choices for customers, and more people will be willing to buy from an industry. California wines for many years had a deserved reputation as usually being inferior to imports. The typical target end user was a skid-row alcoholic. Wines were made as cheaply as possible to provide a lot of alcohol for the buck. When a few vintners began to emulate fine European wines, they knew they had to employ new practices because growing conditions are different in California. By sharing hard-won knowledge with other California wineries, these vintners began to develop fine wines that eventually won acclaim against European wines and established a huge demand for the best California products.

An unexpected benefit of giving away such valuable knowledge is lighting a permanently bigger fire under the company's own efforts to improve. Those added improvements will, in turn, speed industry growth and provide for even more multiplied benefits. In most cases, there's not much to worry about concerning competitive advantage; organizations will be spreading management processes rather than revealing details of proprietary knowledge that's unique to its most valuable offerings.

People vary in how good they are at copying. So it may be necessary for thousands of other organizations to attempt copying the most successful 2,000 percent solution-based organizations before total benefits will expand by another 20 times. That's no problem: The world is full of organizations that would benefit from working on such solutions.

An organization seeking to eventually deliver 64 million times more benefits will normally want to open its doors wide enough to help others copy what it has done in adding revenue, operating cost reductions, capital turnover improvement, reducing capital costs, benefiting stakeholders other than customers and shareholders, and letting copy cats learn from their success in those dimensions. In many cases, the scale for applying the improvements will be even larger in other industries.

A wise master of these dimensions will probably find opportunities to use this sharing to add still more great customers, suppliers, distributors, partners, employees, and sources of new ideas for the company's own activities. It may also be possible to create a joint venture with an educational organization to earn a respectable profit from providing this information.

A good way to begin is to seek publicity about the company's or nonprofit organization's successes. From there, be sure the information-sharing activity can afford appropriate marketing and educational activities to attract and help those who want to copy.

It's also a good idea to work on the learning process so that it can be delivered by using 2,000 percent solutions to speed and to lower the cost for both the company and those who want to copy. Learning these methods will also be helpful for reducing the costs of getting new employees up-to-speed in the company's best ways of making progress.

In sharing those perspectives, I built on some assumptions about human nature. Let me spell out five of the most important assumptions:

1. A highly successful organization will easily shift into complacency and begin devouring many of the benefits of what has already been accomplished unless substantial threats focus attention on making further major improvements.
2. Innovation is accelerated by management becoming more familiar with what is the state of the art.
3. When more people know what the state of the management art is, the state of that art will advance more rapidly.
4. Copying an industry leader or leaders can by highly beneficial to such leaders, much in the same way that supporter and fan behavior can help social leaders improve effectiveness.
5. Choosing innovation paths that benefit from copying allows for multiplied improvements that no single firm could accomplish on its own. As an example, if there had only been one automobile company, today's road and bridge systems would probably be much more limited.

I spell out these assumptions to invite your questions and challenges by e-mail to donmitchell@fastforward400.com/. I also share the assumptions to help you understand that the purpose of stimulating innovation and copying is to expand social benefits by 20 more times in ways that help your organization and its stakeholders by at least that much ... not to provide lots of economic gain for your competitors at the expense of your organization and its stakeholders.

Some might be tempted to dismiss such a broader focus on creating benefits from innovation as being some form of impractical idealism. While many of those who advocate such a broadening of the benefits from innovation base their thinking solely in what matches some personal concept or increases their emotional comfort, *Advanced Business for Innovation: Stimulate Competitor Innovation and Copying* takes its guidance differently. First, direction comes from God's Word, the Bible. Second, insights into how to apply the Bible's wisdom have been gained from the Holy Spirit concerning the many practical ways that encouraging innovation can be good for everyone. Such increased benefits, in turn, can power virtuous cycles of expanding company capabilities, resources, accomplishments, and benefits for sharing that multiply the results with each cycle.

To demonstrate these perspectives concerning innovation, each lesson includes a pertinent selection from the Bible and explains how it applies to stimulating the right behavior and creating vast increases in benefits. The lessons also describe ways that the interests and efforts of companies and their competitors can be so complementary, even without an intention to do so, that any improvements will automatically translate into much more effectiveness and benefits for all.

Let me also explain what I mean by the "value" from innovation. When economists refer to this term, they usually have some utilitarian purpose or dimension in mind. In ordinary speech, of course, value also suggests acquiring something for less: a bargain. In contrast to the first two meanings, we often think of a value as describing what we esteem for guiding our lives, regardless of its current or potential financial worth. While this book often overtly focuses on value in material terms, either owning something that increases in economic worth or acquiring offerings at less cost, the book also advances Biblical values by basing the advice on the perspective of what God values. While we may not know exactly how to measure value in God's terms, we should certainly not pay any less attention to advancing it.

For instance, consider Jesus' words in Matthew 6:24 (NKJV): "No one can serve two masters; for either he will hate the one and love the other, or else he will be loyal to the one and despise the other. You cannot serve God and mammon." (If you aren't familiar with the word *mammon*, it refers in this context to worshiping *riches*, as though they were being personified as a god.) In relating ways to better operate businesses, we should always keep in mind that any such benefits should be directed towards advancing God's Kingdom, rather than some selfish purpose of our own. Otherwise, we will simply be worshiping money rather than God, a terrible sin. We should see using any money developed in this context as simply a means for accomplishing that most important purpose, God's will.

I mention this point now because I have seen variations of some methods described in this book misapplied to violate laws and morality, such as by conspiring with competitors to take advantage of customers and end users. What's the lesson from such applications? I cannot recall seeing any lasting good come from such misdirected uses. So I hope you will apply this information to demonstrate God's greatness to the world and to use the resources He supplies through these methods to glorify Him while serving His purposes.

You should also realize that the laws of each nation differ concerning what actions are permissible for stimulating, contacting, cooperating with, and working with competitors to take certain actions. While undoubtedly each lesson presented in the book is perfectly legal somewhere, any given lesson may not be allowed where you do business. When you believe you know what actions you want to take that are encouraged by this book, I urge you to check with appropriate legal counsel to verify that your plans are wholly acceptable there before taking any actions.

Other 400 Year Project books contain useful guidance for ways to use resources for God's purposes. If you aren't yet familiar with these books, I suggest that you read some or all of them before or while you read and apply this book. A good starting point is *2,000 Percent Living* (Salvation Press, 2010), which describes how to be 20 times more fruitful for the Lord. If you want do delve deeper into the subject of being fruitful, I also suggest *Help Wanted* (2,000 Percent Living Press, 2011). For those who want to focus on witnessing, I recommend *Witnessing Made Easy* (Jubilee Worship Center Step by Step Press, 2010) and *Ways You Can Witness* (Salvation Press, 2010). For anyone who wants to help make a whole nation more fruitful for the Lord, be sure to read and apply *The 2,000 Percent Nation* (400 Year Project Press, 2012).

As you read about the many ways to increase innovation, you may find it helpful to think about how the knowledge could help with expanding and improving a community of believers. Such a reference should increase your focus on making fruitful use of what God provides through these amazing methods, serving to reduce the temptation to use the resources in un-Godly ways.

By implementing all the appropriate lessons from the 50 in *Advanced Business for Innovation: Stimulate Competitor Innovation and Copying* in conjunction with the 50 lessons in *Advanced Business: Exponentially Increase Stakeholder Value* and the 50 lessons for expanding market growth, slashing costs, and eliminating unnecessary investments in *Business Basics* (400 Year Project Press, 2012), a company can increase benefits for its stakeholders by 3.2 million or more times. The next volume in the Advanced Business series, *Advanced Business for Social Benefits*, demonstrates how to build stakeholder value from this impressive level to 64 million or more times through also profiting from serving important social needs. Be sure to read and apply these other value-expanding lessons when they become available!

While some might see these potential gains as either being impossible or not very probable, keep in mind that the for-profit edition of *Excellent Solutions* already provides two improvement processes that can expand stakeholder value by over ten trillion times. In addition, The 400 Year Project has produced such degrees of expanded benefits through the projects of the many people who have applied its God-directed research.

Business Basics, *Advanced Business*, and *Advanced Business for Innovation* can also be used as sources of helpful perspectives and ideas for applying the astonishing value-expanding processes in *Excellent Solutions*. For instance, lessons in *Business Basics* and the Advanced Business series can help identify innovation-encouraging elements to be included in an excellent solution that is developed by using one of the two *Excellent Solutions* processes.

Let me explain other ways to use *Business Basics*, *Advanced Business*, and *Advanced Business for Innovation* to create some of the stakeholder benefits of an excellent solution. If any of the six complementary improvements described in *Business Basics* or the three books in the Advanced Business series' lessons is enhanced for a second time with a new complementary 2,000 percent solution, total stakeholder value would expand by 1.28 billion times. By sequentially improving any one of the six complementary dimensions on four different occasions by 20 times each (or improving for a second time any four of the combined six dimensions by 20 times), total stakeholder value would then grow by 10 trillion times. By expanding performance in these six complementary dimensions through the lessons supplied in these books, most for-profit company leaders would be able to design and implement such large value-improving solutions much more rapidly, with reduced effort, and less expensively than by separately developing ten complementary 2,000 percent solutions to gain the same result.

As I discuss in *Adventures of an Optimist*, two other value dimensions that are partially addressed in *Business Basics*, *Advanced Business*, and *Excellent Solutions* can also be used to complement these six value dimensions:

1. Lower the cost of capital by 96 percent.
2. Engage many underutilized people (such as those who are unemployed or underemployed) in highly productive activities.

Are there any other complementary dimensions that a for-profit company can use as performance enhancements for greatly expanding stakeholder benefits? Yes, I believe that there are many more than just the two dimensions I've just mentioned. I list here two more:

1. Invest in upgrading the skills, knowledge, and resources of many underdeveloped people, especially those with little education and experience, so they can make maximum contributions to all stakeholders and then operate in partnership with those who can, as a result, accomplish still more.
2. Redirect the public's agenda, attention, and resources into improving or increasing highly valuable activities and resources at little cost.

Feel free to add any other complementary performance dimensions that you prefer.

Let me also remind you that while this book is about for-profit businesses, aspects of the discussions about increasing stakeholder benefits through increased innovation are equally, if not more, applicable to nonprofit organizations.

If you have questions or would like to discuss any of these dimensions, processes, or methods, please contact me at my e-mail address, donmitchell@fastforward400.com/.

To make the lessons in this book easier to understand and use, they are divided into four parts, which concern the following topics:

1. Take the initiative to innovate.
2. Improve customer effectiveness.
3. Encourage employees.
4. Stimulate competitors to do more innovating and copying.

I encourage you to direct your colleagues to those parts that will be most relevant to their responsibilities. Doing so will make it easier to redirect your organization's activities in the most fruitful ways.

Let me briefly explain the potential benefits of studying and applying each part. While working with leading organizations that prided themselves on their innovation effectiveness, I was more often struck that these firms were doing more to manage what was happening in the laboratory than to do all of whatever else could be accomplished for increasing innovation. I never detected that these leaders were opposed to doing more activities to enhance innovation, but, rather, that they failed to appreciate most of the opportunities for doing so. In the first part, we help such leaders expand their horizons to appreciate what might be done by one organization to increase innovation by everyone in an industry.

In the second part, we look beyond the organization and its offerings to consider ways to help customers be more effective as a mechanism for increasing the value they receive. Doing so is often the most valuable form of innovation that a company can accomplish. While this part doesn't exhaust this subject, the lessons contain sufficient information to show company leaders the importance of doing more in this regard and some places to start.

In the third part, we move beyond the idea of employees as valuable human resources and stakeholders who should be rewarded by the organization to also seeing the substantial role they can play in developing and conditioning an industry to be much more innovative and effective. For many company leaders, the concepts here will be new.

In the book's final part, we examine activities that your company can encourage that will probably stimulate responses by competitors, viewed solely from their self-interests, to enhance their effectiveness in adding benefits for all stakeholders as innovators and copiers of what you and others do.

By the time you finish reading *Advanced Business for Innovation*, your understanding of what it means to "do business" will have permanently become more fruitful. You will appreciate many new ways your company can use innovation and innovative practices to improve itself, as well as increase the benefits that stakeholders receive. In the process, you'll come to see stimulating competitors to take more beneficial actions as one of your most abundant and inexpensive resources. Shifting to this approach will make you feel as if a large number of people have suddenly begun lifting their fair share of the heavy weight you have been carrying alone: Your burden in increasing innovation will be much less, and you'll be highly encouraged to have so many helpers assisting with bearing any new loads.

Be sure to read the Appendix, as well, where I describe my Christian experiences and testimony. Feel free to share this information with anyone you feel would benefit from learning about how God has touched and improved my life.

We begin in Part One by considering fruitful ways to take the initiative in innovation.

Part One

Take the Initiative to Innovate

Therefore, as through one man's offense
judgment came *to all men,*
resulting in condemnation,

even so through one Man's righteous act
the free gift came *to all men,*
resulting in justification of life.

— Romans 5:18 (NKJV)

Too many times we are inclined to think that an action we might take won't have much effect. We need only recall the sins of Adam and Eve to appreciate that bad actions can have profound and long-lasting effects. For positive effects, we need only consider how Jesus paid the price for our sins, now and forever, on the cross. Although I would be the last person to suggest that an individual could hope to approach what Jesus achieved, please consider times when someone made a big difference in your life. For instance, did someone play a role in helping you understand how to gain Salvation? Did someone decide to accept the free gift of Salvation after you described God's plan through relating the Gospel? Did God answer a prayer that only you made?

While I have no way of knowing of your experiences with a single act making a big difference in your own or someone else's life, I do know that my life has been filled with times when initiatives, those of others and my own, have made huge contributions to advancing God's Kingdom. Some of these instances have been as a private individual, while others have come through the actions of a for-profit or nonprofit organization.

You might think that there are plenty of people who like to innovate, and there certainly are. However, first appreciate that enjoying innovation doesn't mean that you are good at doing it. In addition, realize that there's often a substantial counterpressure to conform and "not make waves" that can inhibit those who can innovate effectively. Further, not all innovation is going to increase benefits. Much attempted innovation will only teach lessons about *what not to do* and *what to do differently next time*. What's my point? *You won't increase the amount of useful innovation unless you take a substantial number of deliberate steps to do so and carefully watch the effects of what you do.*

As the Introduction mentions, most people see innovation too narrowly. While some see innovation opportunities in developing technology, creating new offerings, improving design, and marketing, those are but a few of the many important ways of innovating. In this part, you'll also read about making innovations in business models, processes, stakeholders perceiving benefits, how customers respond, ways competitors behave, and industry structure, among other forms of useful innovation in which you should consider becoming engaged.

While any book containing lessons is, by definition, putting its points in a specific order, let me caution you that the sequence of the lessons in this part may not be optimal for their application by you. However, we begin with a step in Lesson One that I can enthusiastically commend to all readers: Survey and evaluate your company's and the industry's innovation and copying methods. After applying this lesson, you will probably find that some opportunities for taking the initiative to innovate that are described in this part will be more attractive and feasible than others. I encourage you to use what you learn from applying Lesson One to order what steps you take next.

Lesson Two shifts focus to accelerating how often new offerings are introduced. This practice changes customer behavior, increases rewards for your organization's innovations, and makes life more difficult for competitors in ways that should lead to accelerating industry innovation and copying, as well as increasing the benefits that stakeholders receive.

Lesson Three looks at lean innovation, ways to speed, to reduce the cost of, and to enhance the effectiveness of developing major innovations, such as new business models and breakthrough offerings. Doing so becomes a way to discipline an industry by setting a good example of being efficient in innovation, thus causing benefits to expand more rapidly and widely for stakeholders.

In Lesson Four, our focus shifts to putting in place breakthrough business models that competitors can copy. The purpose here is to enhance competitors' effectiveness in ways that will expand Godly benefits for all stakeholders in the industry.

We next look at offering improvements that can be compellingly demonstrated in advertisements, the subject of Lesson Five. When carefully aimed at a modest-sized vulnerability of a competitor that has been reluctant to innovate and to copy, the response should accelerate industry innovation.

For Lesson Six, we look at innovating with superior new offerings that are helped by trends competitors cannot ignore. Such innovations will force the hand of competitors in ways that require becoming faster and better at innovating and copying, especially in finding lower-cost and -priced solutions.

Setting a new standard of user satisfaction that competitors can easily copy is a wonderful way to increase an industry's size and the benefits that are received by all stakeholders. In Lesson Seven, we consider the example of the iPad in establishing a new standard for mobile computing that led to large numbers of copying competitors following Apple.

Our attention shifts in Lesson Eight to providing superior offerings that fill in a line in ways that can be easily copied. Our example focuses on the Mac Air and firms that copied others in the Windows-facilitated PC world.

Lesson Nine takes us to the steel and cloud-storage industries to consider the advantages of first serving customers who demand multiple sources of supply. In the process, the incentives and opportunities for competitors and you to learn from one another will be much greater, undoubtedly leading to much more innovation and copying for adding value for customer and end users.

Lesson Ten explores the possibilities of encouraging competitors to copy so directly that your offerings can substitute for one another, allowing you to endorse the effectiveness of what competitors provide in this regard. This activity can be done in conjunction with or independently of the multiple-sourcing focus of Lesson Nine.

Sometimes competitors won't respond to your encouragement by innovating or copying. When that occurs, you may need to challenge them in ways that will be more likely to be noticed and acted on. Lesson Eleven addresses one way to do so: making improvements that attract a competitors' highest profile customers.

In Lesson Twelve, we look into making good money in attracting competitors' least profitable customers by making profitable innovations. Once again, the purpose is to encourage competitors to innovate or to copy your innovations so that they can retain and attract more of such customers while earning higher profits.

Lesson Thirteen encourages finding ways that competitors' offerings seem dated and adding improvements to your own offerings that increase that perception by adding functional value in new ways. Such a combination will make many competitors feel that they must either innovate or copy your improvements, especially if their biggest and best customers prefer what you have done.

When competitors first begin learning how to copy your innovations, they often won't be very good at doing so. You can help them by making it easier to understand and to duplicate what you've done. Lesson Fourteen explains how to do so.

Lesson Fifteen takes a close look at deliberately omitting expensive features from innovative offerings. After competitive copies become available that include such features, you can then determine which of the features will be worth adding to your next upgrade.

In Lesson Sixteen, our focus shifts to publicly criticizing any competitors whose plans do not include innovating to exceed or copying your innovative offerings. Such criticism will encourage their stakeholders and them to take the opportunities more seriously, potentially changing their plans.

At times, the direct approach works best for stimulating innovation and copying. If other approaches haven't worked, be sure to focus your innovation on a recalcitrant competitor's key strengths, being sure to greatly surpass these advantages in valuable ways. We discuss how to do so in Lesson Seventeen.

Lesson Eighteen looks at the powerful desire felt in many companies to gain so-called bragging rights for accomplishments. By grasping such rights in ways that advance stakeholder needs in Godly ways, you can redirect competitors into innovation and copying that will reinforce what you are doing for the benefit of all.

We then consider the ways that publishing innovation methods and plans can stimulate competitors to be more innovative and better at copying. In the process, we also look at what kind of competitive insulation should be sought so that industry leadership is not lost in the process. These topics are the focus of Lesson Nineteen.

In Lesson Twenty, the advantages of acquiring dominant industry suppliers are explored, with an aim to facilitate increased innovation and copying in the industry for the benefit of all competitors and their stakeholders.

Lesson One

Survey and Evaluate Your Company's and the Industry's Innovation and Copying Methods

Walk as children of light
(for the fruit of the Spirit is in
all goodness, righteousness, and truth),
finding out what is acceptable to the Lord.
And have no fellowship with
the unfruitful works of darkness,
but rather expose them.

— Ephesians 5:8-11 (NKJV)

As Ephesians 5:8-11 (NKJV) tells us, part of our work in advancing God's Kingdom is extending goodness, righteousness, and truth in ways acceptable to Him. In doing so, we often need to identify what is evil, unrighteous, and untruthful about what's going on so that those activities can be exposed as the first step in stopping them. In this lesson, we apply careful investigations and evaluations to the innovation and copying methods that competitors and your organization are using. This work aims at doing more good.

The introduction to Part One observes that business innovation concerns a lot more than developing new technologies, creating new offerings, adding more attractive designs, and applying more effective marketing. For the purposes of this lesson, I also encourage you to consider making innovations in business models, processes, how stakeholders perceive benefits, ways customers respond, influencing competitor behavior, and shifting industry structure, along with any other forms of useful innovation in which you could engage.

The annual audit is a helpful practice for improving accounting in most businesses. An external review by professionals is used to upgrade the accuracy of reports while also strengthening the processes used to generate the numbers that go into such reports. Having recognized the value of doing so for accounting, many companies now also conduct other sorts of annual reviews, often called "audits" as well (although not always with external participants), to check on how well basic activities are being done for everything from strategy to improving the quality of offerings and key processes. However, few organizations conduct such reviews in terms of innovation and copying by competitors. It's time to overcome this lack.

To do so, I suggest asking questions from three different perspectives to identify your organization's most important innovation characteristics:

1. Specifically ask each person who should be aware of innovations to identify and describe any innovations made by your company in technologies, offerings, design, marketing, business models (see *The Ultimate Competitive Advantage*, Berrett-Koehler, 2003, for a discussion of business-model innovation), processes, stakeholder benefits (see the definitions of whom to consider in *Advanced Business: Exponentially Increase Stakeholder Value*, 400 Year Project Press, 2015), ways customers respond, influencing competitor behavior, shifting industry structure, and any other forms of innovation that are thought to be important to your industry or company. Ask each per-

son when the innovations occurred, how the innovations were accomplished, and what the results have been.

2. After receiving the answers, next ask the same people to describe what innovations competitors and other organizations have made during the same time periods that would have been desirable for your organization to have accomplished first.

3. Finally, ask what innovations your organization should have already made that no one has yet achieved in your industry. Then, follow up by asking why such innovations have not yet been accomplished. In doing so, you should begin to spot deficiencies in how your organization approaches innovation.

Where you receive conflicting information about the same examples or types of innovation, do your best to find ways to reconcile what you've learned. Doing so may require following up with more questions and seeking more details. In some cases, it may also be appropriate and comfortable for everyone to meet and discuss the various perspectives. This last approach will work best where you seem to have many bits and pieces of the picture, but cannot yet form them into a coherent overall sense of the issues.

With all of this information available about your organization's past and current innovation activities, you will then be ready to learn about the copying practices used by your competitors, as well as your own organization. In this instance, as well, I suggest that you begin by understanding your organization and quickly develop the contrast with what competitors do. I propose these inquiries be posed to people in your organization, as well as to knowledgeable industry observers:

1. What forms of copying does your organization use to adopt innovations developed by others? Ask for examples and details concerning the methods and effectiveness of these copying methods.

2. What forms of copying do competitors use to copy from your organization's innovations? Again, ask for examples and details.
3. Do other organizations (including those who aren't competitors) use any different methods to copy innovations in and out of your industry?
4. What works well about such copying methods by competitors and other organizations?
5. How could their copying be made more effective?
6. What would be the likely effects of improved copying by competitors in your industry?

With all of this information in hand, it's time to start thinking about the gaps in innovation and copying. Begin to consider what forms of organizational inertia and stalled thinking have contributed to the gaps. Then, start to match missing elements to what is being done now to see how new goals, better information sharing, improved practices, and feeling more competitive heat could accelerate and widen the innovation and copying accomplished by your organization, especially in ways that would bring the greatest stakeholder benefits.

What's the key lesson? *Whether your organization encourages it or not, competitors will seek to innovate and to copy your organization's most successful innovations, especially in new offerings, breakthrough business models, and much enhanced processes. That's just the way most organizations operate. Rather than have the effort potentially create harmful effects for society, your organization, and your stakeholders, you should seek, instead, to encourage innovation and copying that will expand social benefits and push your organization and its stakeholders towards becoming more innovative, as well as better copiers, than would otherwise occur.*

Your Lesson One Assignments

1. Where are your organization's innovation and copying lagging and need to be stimulated?

2. How are competitors innovating and copying what your organization does now?

3. What are the helpful and harmful aspects of such innovation and copying as they exist?

4. How could that innovation and copying be more socially and competitively valuable for your organization and its stakeholders?

5. How could encouraging competitors to innovate more and to copy what you do now stimulate innovation and copying in the areas you identified while working on the first assignment of this lesson?

Lesson Two

Accelerate the Frequency of Introducing New Offerings

And the servant ran to meet her and said,
"Please let me drink a little water from your pitcher."

So she said, "Drink, my lord."

Then she quickly let her pitcher down to her hand,
and gave him a drink.

And when she had finished giving him a drink,
she said, "I will draw water for your camels also,
until they have finished drinking."

Then she quickly emptied her pitcher into the trough,
ran back to the well to draw water,
and drew for all his camels.

— Genesis 24:17-20 (NKJV)

Genesis 24:17-20 (NKJV) demonstrates the importance of quick action when important tasks are at hand. In this chapter of the Old Testament, the patriarch Abraham sends his oldest servant to find a wife for Isaac from among Abraham's own people. On arriving, the servant prays that a woman would help him as a sign of being the wife God had chosen for Isaac. Next, Rebekah arrives and quickly helps with water for the servant and the thirsty camels (a big job!). Her actions convince the servant to offer her Isaac's hand in marriage. Thus, the mother of Jacob was identified. Similarly, when we are doing something of immense importance for God, we must work quickly and well.

Speeding the frequency of introducing new offerings is just such a task. Competitors will have no choice but to copy and to become better at doing so. Knowing that they will soon follow, your own staff will feel a greater urgency to make improvements, especially ones that may bring a little competitive breathing room. Seeing your new behavior, competitors will also feel the need to do more innovating, in addition to their defensive copying.

In many industries, the rate of new offering introductions is irregular. If such introductions are also infrequent, an innovative industry leader will feel little pressure to develop improvements by either innovations or copying. Knowing that it's more profitable and easier just to keep providing more of the same, such an organization can coast and still look good.

Even in such an industry, new offering introductions may not create much of a reaction by competitors if what's changed is mostly minor rather than substantial. Consider the global vehicle market. While almost every vehicle manufacturer announces a new "model" annually for every brand and style, at least five years normally pass before a vehicle is redesigned from the "ground up." Even then, the "new" design may mostly combine existing components from the old or newer models. Is it any wonder that most people aren't going to spend the money to buy a new vehicle when the latest version comes out?

Let's contrast such experiences with providing rapid improvements in performance-related features added to new offerings. To do so, we visit the world of electronic components and software used to generate graphics. NVIDIA chose the role of industry innovator, beginning with developing the Graphic Processing Unit (GPU) in 1999. Since then, the organization sought to bring out a higher performance version for each of its product lines about every six months. Manufacturers and game developers have eagerly awaited the next round of product releases, often using the improvements to provide many experience breakthroughs for end users of games and gaming equipment.

NVIDIA's long-time rival, ATI (now a part of AMD), prospered by copying NVIDIA's innovations and focusing on bringing out low-priced versions of chips and software that were a few product release cycles old. Nintendo, for example, relied on ATI to provide its low-priced Wii games.

The fast pace of performance upgrades fit well with the interests of those gamers who were continually looking for new and more exciting experiences. If you doubt how important such innovations are for electronic games, consider that the market for electronic games and gaming equipment is considerably larger than for the entire motion picture industry, long considered a bellwether of what frequently providing new offerings can do to keep a market lively and growing.

So what happens when an innovation-leading company says it intends to provide frequent major performance upgrades?

First, customers plan their purchasing around such expectations. If a new offering is delayed, sales of the older offerings rapidly decline as many people defer purchasing in anticipation of the next improvements. As you can imagine, expectations of such behavior keep the innovating company focused on finishing its innovations on time and getting them to market.

Second, competitors have a brief window to profitably copy what the innovative leader has just done. The faster copies are available, the sooner and more benefits are received. Notice that the competitors' customers will also delay purchases after your next innovations are available, knowing that they, too, will eventually have something better to purchase from their usual suppliers.

Third, because competitors are in a continual copying race, they will have limited time, attention, and funds available to work on an independent innovation. Their focus will be on simplifying and providing the new benefits less expensively.

Fourth, those who want to work on innovative new offerings will seek jobs at the company bringing out regular offering improvements, while those who want to be efficient copiers will go to work for the competition. As a result, some aspects of innovation may decline among the competitors. You will need to add other programs that deal with that problem, a topic for later lessons.

Fifth, company reputations will reflect such histories. Even if a copying competitor does develop a valuable breakthrough, customers will be skeptical of its existence and may doubt that the innovative streak will continue. The sales force for such a competitor will also lack enough people who know how to sell based on performance rather than on having lower prices.

Sixth, with competitors seeking to do less with fundamental new offerings, the chances are reduced of a mistake occurring by anyone that harms the market's development.

Seventh, you, as the market-leading innovator, also don't have to worry about suffering large market-share losses at the hands of major competitors. Such innovations will come, if at all, from small, narrow-line start-ups.

Granting the importance of such advantages, many organizations will be totally lost in trying to find ways to accelerate the frequency of introducing fundamentally better offerings. That's usually because they are relying on the same people to develop and make available all fundamentally improved offerings. Such an organization needs more bench strength so that those who are capable of delivering highly desirable new offerings have the time and the talented help to do so. If that's not reasonable, external organizations may need to be hired to increase innovation capacity.

Another concern about accelerating the frequency of new offerings may relate to the risk of reduced profitability. If the new offering is actually much more effective or delivers a great many more desirable benefits, customers should be willing to pay more to gain these advantages. As a result, such an innovative company should plan to increase its gross margins to make the cost of such accelerated offering developments more affordable. As you can imagine, such a shift in pricing practices may have to occur gradually over the course of several new offering introductions.

Initially, there's still potential for less profitability. A good way to overcome that problem is by offering contests where the innovations are brought in inexpensively from other industries, a subject covered in much detail by the lessons in *Advanced Business*. Lessons Forty-Four through Forty-Nine in this book look at increasing innovation through similar contests.

Some companies may be concerned about identifying what new benefits to provide ... or finding ways to deliver such benefits. Clearly, a longer-term vision is needed of what the market lacks in order to grow faster and larger. If an organization doesn't have such a capability, it will need to hire organizations to help in this regard or to beef up its internal activities for appreciating what customers and end users will buy if made available. The Billionaire Entrepreneurs' Master Mind's work on how to expand a market can be of great help in this regard. You will find useful ideas among the first lessons in *Business Basics*.

Avoid mistakenly focusing on providing the wrong benefits. When gasoline prices are soaring is no time to introduce a larger, fuel-guzzling SUV with a bigger V-8 engine. Where there's a long delay between defining new offerings and actually providing them, such problems can occur.

To overcome such risks, it's best to shorten the length of the development cycle. After as much has been done as is possible in this regard, also hedge a company's bets by providing multiple new offerings that cover a wider range of the potential spectrum of benefits that customers, end users, and other stakeholders may be seeking.

Then, some of the performance improvements are bound to be right for whatever market environment is encountered.

What's the key lesson? *An industry leader that accelerates its new offering introduction frequency can be highly productive in expanding a market faster, increasing the rate of its own innovations, and reducing exposure to harm by mistaken innovations provided by its competitors.*

Your Lesson Two Assignments

1. What kind of benefits can you provide more of in future offerings that will accelerate market growth, reduce stakeholder costs, eliminate stakeholder investments, and increase value for stakeholders?

2. Is your organization capable of developing such new offering benefits on its own?

3. Who else can help accelerate innovation involving such useful benefits?

4. How often can your organization afford to develop such fundamentally improved new offerings?

5. If you develop such new offering benefits, will competitors be willing to copy you?

6. How long will be the lag between your first making the offering available and competitors providing copies?

7. If your organization cannot afford to make such developments as rapidly as would be desirable, are partners and other stakeholders willing to join with you in this activity?

8. How else can your new offering development processes and activities be changed to accelerate the rate of your organization's innovations?

Lesson Three

Apply Lean Innovation

'Therefore thus says the Lord GOD to them:

"Behold, I Myself will judge between
the fat and the lean sheep.
Because you have pushed with side and shoulder,
butted all the weak ones with your horns,
and scattered them abroad,
therefore I will save My flock,
and they shall no longer be a prey;
and I will judge between sheep and sheep.

"I will establish one shepherd over them,
and he shall feed them — My servant David.
He shall feed them and be their shepherd.
And I, the LORD, will be their God,
and My servant David a prince among them;
I, the LORD, have spoken."'

— Ezekiel 34:20-24 (NKJV)

In Ezekiel 34:20-24 (NKJV), God chastises the leaders of Israel for using those they lead to feather the leaders' nests, rather than serving the people to make them safer and stronger. God makes it clear that in abandoning their duty to properly shepherd the sheep (the people of Israel), the leaders have lost their claim to this role and to His favor. A new leader will replace them, Jesus Christ, with God the Father blessing the people. From this example, we can see that business leaders should also do more with the resources that God provides so that stakeholders are better taken care of. Innovation guided by the Holy Spirit is clearly one of the most important ways that business leaders can be faithful to their charge from God. Lean innovation can be a helpful method for doing so.

This lesson considers a specific way of accelerating innovation that is likely to stimulate a flurry of competitive copying. Encouraging such copying is important because otherwise there will be fewer benefits and your organization could easily be caught up in the pride of seeking to impress others.

Before explaining more about this management process for innovation, let me refer you to a book by Eric Ries, *The Lean Startup* (Crown Business, 2011), that explains several aspects of accelerated innovation in ways that make the process much easier for you and your organization to understand and to use. The idea's essence is to identify assumptions that lie behind a business model and intended offerings, and then to test if those assumptions are correct in very rapid, low-cost ways. Often this testing is done by first creating a minimal version of the offering and business model that is sufficient to let potential customers react to what you are planning. For instance, an elaborate new software program might be demonstrated by a brief video showing what it would be like to work with the software without actually building any software. Simulated computer screens could be used make the simulation seem more "real."

In most cases, such testing would be based on minimal versions of potential new offerings that are created in hours or days for a few hundred dollars. Each iteration of testing should build on what was learned from reactions to the last simulation.

At the point when a viable offering and business model appear to exist, actual offerings can begin to be provided. In the early stages, such versions might appear to the customer to be finished offerings, but in reality they would usually be based on custom work having been done that customers haven't paid for and didn't realize was occurring. The idea is to learn from seeing what customers do with the actual offerings ... and continually make changes until something very good is found that's worth turning into a low-cost version of the benefit.

Such innovation should also emphasize testing the market response based on daily metrics for those customers who are first introduced to the offering. Let me explain what I mean by a hypothetical example.

Let's assume we are talking about a Web site that offers free information supported by advertising revenues ... but a site that also provides paid services. The daily metrics might look at how many people visit the site, the percentage of visitors that download anything from the site, and the percentage of those who download anything that purchase a paid service. Each day's results would then provide comparable data to prior and later days to show how well any innovations in the Web site, marketing, and the services offered affect attracting visitors, active visitors, and paying users.

By deliberately splitting what potential and actual visitors see into subsets of all those who are contacted in a day, with enough visitors an organization can test potentially hundreds of new iterations each day to see how the key metrics improve or decline from the best prior performance. As a result, more learning might occur in one day than would happen over decades at a company using only conventional innovation methods.

Here's where the beauty of the method comes in for competitor copying: Competing organizations now face in your organization a firm that moves at what will seem like light speed in making improvements and breakthroughs compared to what a typical organization does. In such a situation, most competing organizations would conclude that their best course is to carefully monitor what you are rolling out and to follow as rapidly as possible with identical offerings at a slightly lower price. As a consequence, market growth will be greatly increased and scale effects achieved much sooner for everyone in the industry. The better the copying that occurs, the greater will be your organization's incentive to look at totally new business models and breakthrough offerings, avoiding the sloth that often follows from only seeking to make incremental improvements.

As you can imagine, your organization is also greatly helped by being able to make subtle adjustments that will be too delicate and hard to observe for a competitor to precisely copy. As a result, your "original" innovation and its rapid follow-on versions will always seem superior to current and potential customers.

If what you provide is tricky or expensive to do correctly, it's also a good idea to apply lean operating methods (such as those based on the famous Toyota manufacturing system) to produce and to deliver your offerings to customers. Such methods are also good for reducing costs, increasing flexibility, and eliminating the need for many kinds of investments.

What's the key lesson? *An industry-leading organization that sincerely wants to accelerate useful innovation can be helped by making it easier for its own organization to learn and to innovate by applying lean innovation ... forcing competitors to become better at rapid copying at lower costs and prices, thus setting the bar higher for what the leading organization will will need to accomplish for itself in future innovations.*

Your Lesson Three Assignments

1. How could you and your stakeholders benefit because you make it easier for your organization to focus on identifying what it needs to learn, acquiring that knowledge much faster and less expensively, and providing an incentive for competitors to follow your big successes very rapidly?

2. What would have to change about your innovation priorities, budgets, processes, and practices if competitors become more effective copiers of your best offerings?

3. How could you use increasing the supply of innovations and making it easier for competitors to succeed in copying as an advantage in stimulating your future innovations?

4. What could you do now to encourage making valuable innovations available much sooner from your organization ... beyond what lean innovation methods can provide?

5. How can you prepare in advance to make any gains in increasing competitors' copying from accelerating your own innovation even more productive for your organization, your stakeholders, and the industry?

Lesson Four

Create Breakthrough Business Models Competitors Can Copy

*The Philistines also went and
deployed themselves in the Valley of Rephaim.*

*So David inquired of the LORD, saying,
"Shall I go up against the Philistines?
Will You deliver them into my hand?"*

*And the LORD said to David,
"Go up, for I will doubtless deliver
the Philistines into your hand."*

*So David went to Baal Perazim,
and David defeated them there;*

*and he said,
"The LORD has broken through
my enemies before me,
like a breakthrough of water."*

*Therefore he called the name
of that place Baal Perazim.*

— 2 Samuel 5:18-20 (NKJV)

These verses from 2 Samuel 5 (NKJV) teach us that while humans can always scheme to do something different, a true breakthrough that leads to the right kind of victory comes only with God's permission and direction. While a new business model (different ways of providing offerings in terms of what you do, who you do it with, for whom you do it, how you do it, when it's done, where you accomplish the results, and how much it all costs) can be easily envisioned, many such ideas won't bear fruit because they don't advance God's Kingdom. So in addition to studying 400 Year Project books (such as *The Ultimate Competitive Advantage* in this case), be sure to follow King David's example and inquire of the Lord about a potential new business model to determine if you are to engage in it and, if so, to find out how you should, as well as to publicly praise Him for the results.

As background for this lesson, I made a careful study of the life of Steve Jobs, primarily relying on the biography, *Steve Jobs*, by Walter Isaacson (Simon & Schuster, 2011). If you haven't yet read the book, I highly recommend it as a source of information about Steve Jobs and innovation at Apple and Pixar.

As I read, I was struck by Steve Jobs' passion not to compromise what he thought was important. In taking that approach, he often insisted on creating business-model breakthroughs that would not otherwise have been made. Once the new business model was in place, competitors could see ways to copy what Apple or Pixar had just created. As a result, Apple or Pixar then needed to again innovate to establish a new lead.

Let me give you an example of what Jobs did to make our investigation more concrete. Two big hurdles had been holding back customers from purchasing electronic music:

1. Music publishers' insistence that whole albums be purchased, even if a customer only wanted to listen to a single cut from an album

2. Difficult, time-consuming downloads of electronic music that provided poor quality sound reproduction for the effort

Although Apple viewed itself as a provider of experiences, Jobs appreciated that a utility was needed to overcome these two big hurdles: the iTunes store that would allow inexpensive, quick, easy to access, high quality downloads of individual cuts of music. Typically, a hardware manufacturer would see such a limitation in terms of software and either write some or encourage suppliers to do so.

If Apple had taken the familiar route, its iTunes store would simply have allowed people to easily and quickly download high quality versions of whole albums at the usual prices. Such an "innovation" wouldn't have changed the industry very much. Competitors might not have even bothered to copy it.

Apple focused first on convincing music publishers to offer individual cuts at 99 cents and to pay Apple 30 percent of that amount. A few years earlier, music publishers probably wouldn't have paid attention. But they had been steadily losing potential sales due to customers simply exchanging purchased music with one another, either informally or on Web sites that facilitated such exchanges. Facing the potential loss of most payments for recorded music, music publishers reluctantly agreed to Jobs' thinking that they should make available purchases of high quality electronic music easier to do, flexible, and less expensive.

The rest is history. Apple drove device sales by making the iTunes store compatible with all of its devices, from iPods to desktop iMacs to iPhones to iPads. If you didn't have such a device, Apple also opened its store to personal computer users.

Since then, the iTunes store has expanded into providing ways to purchase, store, and view television programs, videos, and movies on all the Internet-connected devices a customer owns.

Apple has two substantial rivals for these customers: Google with its Android operating system for mobile devices and Amazon with its Kindle line of electronic book readers. Both Google and Amazon had bigger plans, which included selling content as a major way to profit from providing portable devices and related applications.

Because Apple had already established the model for how device makers and software writers could partner with music publishers, Google and Amazon were able to establish their own music stores using the same pricing and revenue-sharing models. While Amazon might well have pulled off such a concept eventually on its own, it's clear that Amazon's expansion into portable devices and electronic media of all kinds has been greatly accelerated by Apple's negotiating breakthrough with music publishers.

As a result, Apple has succeeded in helping to attract two substantial competitors who will push it to keep making breakthroughs if it is to stay ahead of the innovations that both Google and Amazon are capable of making on their own. As an example, I was amused to see a Kindle notebook disassembled and evaluated on a business television program one day. Almost all of the components were identical to the ones that Apple was using in its iPad.

There's no doubt that Apple employees will feel future innovation pressure from such strong competitors that will probably be almost as intense as having Steve Jobs shouting at them to make more breakthrough improvements. It's a wonderful legacy from the deceased innovator.

So what are the lessons for you? Focus on these four elements:

1. Create breakthrough business models or business-model elements that competitors would not otherwise be able to produce on their own.
2. Leave the door open for competitors to produce roughly comparable business models or business-model elements.
3. Make the economics highly attractive to new entrants and to those who specialize in different ways to compete.
4. Continue to compete by making further differentiations that solve important problems that still discourage customers and end users.

What's the key lesson? *An industry-leading organization that sincerely wants to accelerate useful innovation can be helped by creating breakthrough business models that competitors can copy ... forcing competitors to become better at rapid copying at lower prices, thus setting the bar higher for what the leading organization will need to seek to accomplish for itself in future breakthrough business-model innovations that competitors can copy.*

Your Lesson Four Assignments

1. How could you and your stakeholders benefit because you make business-model breakthroughs that competitors and strong entrants can copy, providing an incentive for competitors to simply follow your big successes in this regard very rapidly?

2. What would have to change about your innovation priorities, budgets, processes, and practices if competitors become more effective copiers of your business-model breakthroughs?

3. How could you use creating breakthrough business models that competitors can easily copy as an advantage in stimulating your future innovations?

4. What could you do now to encourage making valuable innovations available much sooner from your organization ... beyond what creating breakthrough business models that competitors can copy will provide?

5. How can you prepare in advance to make any gains in increasing competitors' copying from creating breakthrough business models even more productive for your organization, your stakeholders, and the industry?

Lesson Five

Make Offering Improvements That Can Be Compellingly Demonstrated in Advertising

For scarcely for a righteous man will one die;
yet perhaps for a good man
someone would even dare to die.
But God demonstrates His own love toward us,
in that while we were still sinners,
Christ died for us.
Much more then, having now been justified
by His blood, we shall be saved
from wrath through Him.

— Romans 5:7-9 (NKJV)

While arguments can be made in favor of almost anything, we only occasionally find proof so compelling that anyone who considers it will be persuaded. God sending His Son Jesus to die for us so that our souls might be saved is such compelling proof of love that only those who reject the very existence of God and His Son can deny the worthiness of this sacrifice. The gift is so great and so wonderful that billions of people have chosen to believe in and act on it.

By contrast, business advertisements usually look good, but do not say very much beyond appealing to our vanity, seldom demonstrating anything we haven't seen pretty much everywhere else. In such a context, imagine how much more impressive an offering improvement would be that could be clearly seen in advertising as being advantageous over the alternatives.

While such an approach can clearly gather a lot of customers and improve a business, doing so can also trigger much greater industry innovation. Let me explain.

You may sometimes face situations where it makes more sense to "nudge" a competitor into copying rather than to "bulldoze" a copycat reaction. One possible example is where your competitor's unit is smaller than yours, but the unit is part of a much larger organization with substantial resources that could potentially swamp your own organization's capabilities and means.

In such a circumstance, it would be better to "encourage" the competitor to start copying ... rather than to have a competitor feel "threatened."

How might such encouragement be provided? Rather than attacking the competitors' biggest vulnerability, you would choose to undermine a medium-sized vulnerability.

You might start out by surveying a sample of your competitor's customers to find out why each one buys from the competitor rather than from your organization. Focus on questions related to the offerings, rather than other kinds of differences between you and the competitor.

From the survey, you should be able to estimate the volume each offering represents to the competitor. By reverse engineering the competitor's offerings, you should also be able to estimate profit contribution per unit. Combine the apparent volumes with the survey answers for what different characteristics provide in volume and profit contribution. Then, pick some aspect of the competitor's advantages that represents between 5 and 15 percent of total profit contribution. That's the size of advantage that you should consider leapfrogging past.

Before fixing on a particular competitive advantage to overcome and to turn into a disadvantage for the competitor, you also need to think about what kind of a demonstration you could put into a print ad (if that's the only way you advertise now), a radio spot (if that's one of the major media you advertise in now), or a television commercial (if that's how you most often advertise).

You want a demonstration to put into an ad that's so compelling that no one other than the owner's mother would continue to use the competitor's offering after seeing it.

What kind of a demonstration can make a big splash? Before I could think of any business examples, I was immediately reminded of two other Biblical ones: Jesus rising from the dead after three days and being seen by hundreds of people over the next forty days, and the Hebrews being led by a pillar of fire at night and a cloud during the daytime while miraculously receiving manna six days a week during forty years in the desert. Anyone seeing either of those circumstances would have had a hard time not believing in God, His presence, and His superiority over other so-called gods. Even thousands of years later, just reading the testimonies of people who observed these events compels many people to believe in Him.

In business, there have been some notable advertising demonstrations. I'm reminded of the Crest toothpaste advertisements during the times when there were no other toothpastes containing fluoride. Crest did split family and split school tests where half of each group used their regular toothpaste and half used Crest. The clinical differences in cavities were reported, and happy Crest users appeared in the ads to endorse Crest. It wasn't long before almost all toothpastes in the United States added fluoride. You may be interested to know that fluoride was very controversial in those days. Many cities and towns refused to add it to their water supplies because of ill-founded concerns about health risks. Thus, the demonstrations were also there, in part, to change public opinion about the benefits of fluoride.

Another famous example is the blind comparison taste test conducted by Pepsi-Cola where the majority of consumers picked Pepsi-Cola as tasting better than Coca-Cola. Market share began to quickly shift toward Pepsi-Cola. In a panic, Coca-Cola developed a new formulation that negated most of its taste disadvantage by adding more sugar and carbonation. Quickly developed and launched, the so-called New Coke did well for a few weeks until the original Coke was withdrawn. When that happened, Coke drinkers were livid. Coke then brought back the original Coke as Coke Classic. Within two years, sales of New Coke were little more than zero, and the product was ultimately discontinued. But the advertisements were clearly wonderful for prodding Coca-Cola to copy Pepsi-Cola.

What's the key lesson? *An industry-leading organization that sincerely wants to accelerate its useful innovations can be helped by making offering improvements versus competitors that can be compellingly demonstrated in advertising so that competitors will feel required to copy.*

Your Lesson Five Assignments

1. How could you and your stakeholders benefit because you make offering improvements that can be compellingly demonstrated in advertising?

2. After you put in offering improvements that can be compellingly demonstrated in advertising, what would have to change about innovation priorities, budgets, processes, and practices to encourage such future accomplishments?

3. How could you use offering improvements that can be compellingly demonstrated in advertising as an advantage in stimulating your future innovations?

4. What else could you do now to encourage making valuable innovations available much sooner from your organization ... beyond adding offering improvements versus competitors that can be compellingly demonstrated in advertising?

5. How can you prepare in advance to make more innovation gains by increasing competitors' copying from making improvements that can be compellingly demonstrated in advertising?

Lesson Six

Develop Superior Offerings Helped by Trends That Competitors Will Be Sure to Notice

And her mother-in-law said to her,
"Where have you gleaned today?
And where did you work?
Blessed be the one who took notice of you."

So she told her mother-in-law
with whom she had worked, and said,
"The man's name with whom
I worked today is Boaz."

Then Naomi said to her daughter-in-law,
"Blessed be he of the LORD,
who has not forsaken His kindness
to the living and the dead!"

And Naomi said to her,
"This man is a relation of ours,
one of our close relatives."

— Ruth 2:19-20 (NKJV)

In Ruth 2:19-20 (NKJV), we see the results of doing the right thing, in this case Ruth following her mother-in-law to a land that was not her own and unselfishly serving Naomi there. Ruth's righteousness attracted the attention of Boaz who later became her second husband, and through this marriage Ruth entered into line of Jesus' forbearers despite being a Gentile. The book of Ruth demonstrates how God can use the good things we do to advance His Kingdom.

Businesses developing superior offerings that benefit from trends no competitor can ignore will probably attract attention, as Ruth did, for having done something appropriate. Action by observers will follow in such cases, as with Boaz.

As with Lesson Four, this lesson is informed by the biography, *Steve Jobs*, by Walter Isaacson. As I read the book, I was struck by Steve Jobs' vision concerning the future of computing. For some time, he correctly believed that many people would be using a variety of devices throughout the day, whether at an office, at home, or somewhere else. Clearly, some of these devices would have to be highly mobile, while some could be quite static in their placement, such as a desktop computer.

However, Jobs anticipated that the same person would want to easily access the same records, software, and entertainment on all of these devices. While the Internet clearly could make such universal access possible, the required applications would be more seamless and convenient if they were part of a closed system intended to serve this purpose. And so Steve Jobs began to create such a system with the iMac and the iPod as his first two devices, later adding the iPhone and iPad.

While it was obvious to most people that computing was going to become quite mobile, far fewer people appreciated the ultimate desire for seamless interoperability among many kinds of devices. By establishing that standard, Apple's competitors could quickly see it would **become an essential element in user** decisions about what equipment, software, and content to purchase.

How hard was it to anticipate this trend? I don't think it was hard at all. Television sets provided a clue. While most American homes had only one or two television sets in 1975, it was not unusual for there to be five to seven as of 1995. As video recordings and cable-television offerings became more available, people wanted to continue watching something as they moved from room to room doing their normal activities. Thus, a viewing begun in the living room might continue in the kitchen while preparing a meal. To make continual viewing possible, electronics manufacturers early on provided ways for cable services and DVR players to share a feed into different televisions throughout a house.

In contrast with the alternative of establishing industry standards as a way to encourage such copying, in this case a company standard was established without consultation with competitors in order to define a superior customer experience. The success of the approach, combined with the obvious trend, then drove competitors to create their own substitutes ... through software, cloud computing, and greater Web-site capabilities.

This approach to encouraging copying is clearly going to be superior in a circumstance where competitors are unlikely to desire setting a standard as early as a market-leading company might want, the market-leading company wants to gain an advantage over the competitors, or there are likely to be major disagreements among industry participants.

While I have undertaken no investigation into how this circumstance was addressed by others, I believe I can draw five suggested guidelines for how to apply this lesson's principle from the Apple example:

1. Look at the interaction of two or more major trends that are highly likely to continue for a long time.
2. Find ways to establish major advantages for stakeholders that could not be easily duplicated by negotiating new industry standards.

3. Leave open some paths for competitors to duplicate or to exceed your solutions.
4. Be prepared to fulfill the demand from any accelerated industry growth that occurs so that stakeholders who prefer what you offer won't be burdened by inferior solutions.
5. Build your solution to reward those who embrace it early and continue with it. That approach will compel competitors to do more to attract people who use your offerings, stimulating innovative solutions that will drive your organization to be, once again, highly inventive in delivering still better solutions.

What's the key lesson? *An industry-leading organization that sincerely wants to accelerate useful innovation can be helped by developing superior offerings competitors can copy that are helped by trends competitors are sure to notice ... forcing competitors to become better at rapid copying at lower costs and prices, thus setting the bar higher for what a leading organization will need to accomplish for itself in innovative future offerings helped by trends that competitors will be sure to notice.*

Your Lesson Six Assignments

1. How could you and your stakeholders benefit because you develop superior offerings that competitors and strong entrants can copy that are helped by trends competitors will be sure to notice, providing an incentive for competitors to very rapidly follow your big successes in this regard?

2. What would have to change about your innovation priorities, budgets, processes, and practices if competitors become more effective copiers of your superior offerings that are helped by trends that competitors will be sure to notice?

3. How could you use developing superior offerings competitors can easily copy that are helped by trends competitors will be sure to notice as an advantage in stimulating your future innovations?

4. What could you do now to encourage making valuable innovations available much sooner from your organization ... beyond what developing superior offerings helped by trends that competitors will be sure to notice will provide?

5. How can you prepare in advance to make any gains in increasing competitors' copying by developing superior offerings helped by trends even more productive for your organization, your stakeholders, and the industry?

Lesson Seven

Set a New Standard of User Satisfaction

The fear of the LORD leads to life,
And he who has it will abide in satisfaction;
He will not be visited with evil.

— Proverbs 19:23 (NKJV)

Many people mistakenly seek temporary pleasure as a means of gaining lasting satisfaction. Proverbs 19:23 (NKJV) makes it clear that following God's plan is the reliable road to a life of continuing satisfaction, one free from evil influences. While business offerings cannot hope to cause similar levels and duration of satisfaction, leaders should continually strive to upgrade the standard of satisfaction provided for those who use their offerings. While doing so, a wise organization will also encourage belief in God, His Son, and the Holy Spirit so that more people can gain the true source of satisfaction.

As were lessons four and six, this lesson is also informed by *Steve Jobs* by Walter Isaacson. I was fascinated by how Apple's innovations quickly attracted copying competitors who often brought their own innovations to the market. For example, soon after the iPad come out, hundreds of notebook computers were made available with reasonably similar characteristics.

What was this reaction about? Unless you are a notebook computer historian, you may not remember that the iPad was not Apple's first foray into highly portable computing. Its previous entry was the Newton, a tablet computer. Unlike the more recent notebook computers, tablet computers reduced their size by providing a stylus that enabled users to input data. Tablet computers relied on handwriting recognition software that was supposed to "learn" by deciphering more of a user's writing. Unfortunately, the software wasn't all that great. The main lesson gained from the 1993 tablet computers was that a keyboard works far better than a stylus for inputting.

The implications of that learning, however, weren't captured at Apple until well after the return of Steve Jobs to Apple in 1996. Naturally, Jobs had bigger opportunities to attract his attention than notebook computing, especially since he realized that many component, hardware, and software improvements were needed before notebooks could be decent alternatives to laptops.

Jobs eventually returned to facilitating mobile computing, beginning work on the iPad before the iPhone. However, Apple noted that the technical solutions the company developed would work even better for a phone than for a notebook computer. As a result, internal priorities were shifted toward first launching the iPhone.

The iPad soon followed. Since both devices employed similar technology, were easy to use, and made mobile computing much more attractive, the iPhone caused there to be much more interest in and understanding of the iPad's advantages. As a consequence, sales grew faster for both devices.

Why did so much copying occur? The market for mobile computing on cell phones had long been forecast to become huge, and the faster development of this market in Europe and Japan than in North America validated many consumer preferences. Competitors and potential entrants who saw the iPhone then decided to produce their own versions. Many of them also realized that there would be good demand for notebook computers among users who wanted the benefits of portability with a larger screen than would be offered by a cell phone with computing capabilities.

The effect of having so many notebook computing introductions at about the same time also meant that those who wanted to do mobile computing could see that they could accomplish much of what they wanted in connection with the Internet by using a notebook computer rather than a laptop. The advantages in portability convenience due to lighter weight and smaller size meant that most people would prefer a notebook over a laptop or a cell phone connected to the Internet for looking at images, watching videos, having visual "chats," taking notes, and doing large amounts of messaging.

Because graphic user interfaces (GUIs) were so well established and highly regarded by that time, anyone who wanted to offer a notebook computer needed to use that method, make the devices safe and reliable, and pick a price lower than Apple's. A copycat market was soon born that was built around the new standard of user satisfaction.

You may remember that graphics for gaming has been another electronic market where increased standards of user satisfaction were continually being provided by the market leader, NVIDIA. Those who wanted the most intense gaming experiences would always use products containing the latest NVIDIA graphic-processing chip. Suppliers of such equipment and games could charge a large price premium for them. Those who were satisfied with less intense experiences would gladly purchase equipment and games that featured slightly out-of-date technology at much lower prices. Soon thereafter, other graphic processing computers would deliver their own products that mimicked the new standard initially provided by NVIDIA.

The challenge in taking this approach is, of course, that the new standard has to produce superior user satisfaction. The iPad did ... and the Newton didn't. Two methods can be helpful in making such a judgment concerning superior user satisfaction before beginning to spend time, money, and effort to provide the new "standard:"

1. Create a simulation of the benefits to let users experience the new standard and observe their reactions. In doing so, be sure to use a simulation that's pretty close to the performance you can actually deliver, rather than a "perfect" result when you will initially deliver only 30 percent of that standard.
2. Use panels of technical experts to evaluate what's feasible to deliver at what price with the new standard. It's important to overcome unwarranted optimism and pessimism to develop more realistic views. I well remember working with a company in the early 1980s that had a contract to write software that would allow a Macintosh computer to operate PC software. The contract was tied to what Apple wanted to spend rather than to a realistic amount (which was more than 15 times larger). Naturally, the project was a flop, and the time, money, and effort were wasted. Stung by this experience, Apple delayed making the necessary changes, losing millions of Macintosh unit sales during the years when it had large disadvantages in application software.

To ensure copying you'll also have to either license your intellectual property or not seek any legal rights to exclusivity for your breakthrough. In most cases, the licensing route will be advantageous. But the other route can make more sense when you want to attract new entrants from among large potential competitors that aren't usually going to be interested in serving the same market. That's what Apple did by leaving the door open for Amazon to design a version of its market-leading Kindle readers that can also function as a notebook competitor for Apple and its traditional rivals.

Finally, you also need to leave competitors with hope that the copying door will remain open at a reasonable cost to them so that they will be able to meeting higher future standards. Then, you'll see the anticipation of expanded sales from increased user satisfaction draw copying competitors like bees to pollen-laden flowers.

What's the key lesson? *An industry-leading organization that sincerely wants to accelerate its useful innovations can be helped under certain circumstances through upgrading its offerings to set a new, higher standard of user satisfaction that competitors can quickly and easily copy.*

Your Lesson Seven Assignments

1. How could you and your stakeholders benefit because you upgrade offerings to set a new, higher standard of user satisfaction that competitors can quickly and easily copy?

2. What would have to change about your innovation priorities, budgets, processes, and practices if competitors become more effective copiers of your upgraded offerings that have just set a new, higher standard of user satisfaction?

3. How could you use developing higher standards of user satisfaction and letting competitors copy you as an advantage in stimulating your future innovations?

4. What else could you do now to encourage making valuable innovations available much sooner from your organization ... beyond setting a new, higher standard of user satisfaction that competitors can quickly and easily copy?

5. How can you prepare in advance to make any gains in increasing competitors' copying by setting a new, higher standard of user satisfaction even more productive for your organization, your stakeholders, and the industry?

Lesson Eight

Fill Out Your Offering Line With Easy to Copy Items

"A new commandment I give to you,
that you love one another;
as I have loved you,
that you also love one another."

— John 13:34 (NKJV)

At the Last Supper, Jesus prepared His disciples for the trials to come leading to His crucifixion, as well as to the wonder of His resurrection from the dead. However, His theme wasn't so narrow. Instead, Jesus encouraged the disciples to be copiers of Him in loving one another. To me, it's just another sign of how great His love is, in that He wanted us to learn to love in the way that He does. Similarly, we should help our competitors to succeed by being sure that whatever we offer contains at least some items that are easy for them to copy, as a way of helping them to become better innovators.

Once again, as were lessons four, six, and seven, this lesson also draws, in part, on material from *Steve Jobs* by Walter Isaacson. During a visit to an Apple store, I was struck by the design, slimness, and light weight of the MacBook Air, an ultrabook computer. Designed to be as powerful as a desktop or a typical laptop computer for most applications, the Air weighed much less and was thinner. If you are always on the go and need to compute a great deal, the latest version of the Air could be a great alternative.

This product fills a need for those who value portability and ease of use, and require many more capabilities than netbooks and tablet computers provide, especially for those who want a full keyboard and touch pad. The upgraded versions of the Air have as much battery life as a notebook computer.

Seeing the Air reminded me of the early days of General Motors when the company added a number of brands by acquisition to include products at more price points with widely varying features so that buyers could pick almost any combination they wanted of prestige, image, features, and price.

Because the Air is based on an Intel chip, it was only a matter of time before Intel decided that this type of product was a major opportunity and brought out a line of chips just for ultrabooks (the trademarked name for products using Intel's new chips) that can be used with Windows operating systems. After the chips were available, many ultrabooks were introduced.

After all those ultrabooks were developed, Air sales also increased as more people considered whether to get an ultrabook ... rather than the less expensive desktop and laptop computers. Whenever that happened within the Apple line, it was a highly profitable trade-up for Apple. In the process, these users found that they wanted still more battery life, a still slimmer profile, more styling, and greater functionality in applications such as gaming. Naturally, Apple then brought out a series of upgraded products that better met such needs, causing an upgrade cycle to start prior to the newly acquired gear actually being filled to its capacity.

So what will stimulate your customers to buy and end users to employ a new offering, as well as for competitors to copy it?

Begin by scanning your line of offerings to see if there are places between your offerings where you could offer added combinations of price, functionality, and performance that would be valuable to a significant percentage of current customers and end users in that space.

Next, consider how you might supply those benefit combinations in ways that are profitable now ... or would become decently profitable within a short period of time.

After that, look into what the upgrade path might look like for those who are willing to try your new line fillers.

Focus on the opportunities that are largest for immediate trial and long-term upgrades through adding more features at modest cost for the value of what is to be provided (either through offering redesign or including the benefit of technology advances).

Consider how having competitors copy your line fill-ins would help establish credibility for what you want to do and more interest in considering your offerings.

Price your initial line fill-ins high enough such that competitors will feel a strong desire to copy what you provide, even if their sales volumes turn out to be low.

Avoid putting any limits on suppliers helping competitors with copying.

Don't put intellectual property limits in place on copying that could delay the copies becoming available or make providing them functionally impractical.

Get ready then for a race to upgrade customers and end users from these fill-in offerings into many future generations of improved choices!

What's the key lesson? *An industry-leading organization that sincerely wants to accelerate its useful innovations can be helped by filling in any offering-line gaps with superior offerings that can be easily and quickly copied and upgraded.*

Your Lesson Eight Assignments

1. How could you and your stakeholders benefit because your competitors can quickly and easily copy your newest offering-line fill-ins?

2. If competitors become more effective copiers of your fill-in offerings, what would have to change about your innovation priorities, budgets, processes, and practices?

3. How could you use fill-in offerings as an advantage in stimulating your future innovations?

4. What else could you do now to encourage making valuable innovations available much sooner from your organization ... beyond making it easy for competitors to copy your fill-ins?

5. How can you prepare in advance to make any increases in competitors' copying from making it easy for competitors to emulate your fill-in offerings even more productive for your organization, your stakeholders, and the industry?

Lesson Nine

Focus on Customers
Who Demand Multiple Sources

But they were insistent,
demanding with loud voices
that He be crucified.

And the voices of these men and of
the chief priests prevailed.

— Luke 23:23 (NKJV)

When a group of people insists on something, everyone else will often have to give way. In the case of Jesus, as described in Luke 23 (NKJV), Pilate did not want to crucify Jesus. However, the insistent voices demanding this cruel punishment eventually swayed Pilate, and Jesus was headed to the cross to fulfill God's plan for our Salvation.

Customers can often be a lot more rational in making their demands. Be sure to pay attention when they insist. It's usually easier for them to just go elsewhere, rather than to tell you what you need to do.

When what you provide is absolutely essential to a customer or end user and your own organization is relatively small compared to them, many customers and end users will insist on purchasing what you offer from more than one supplier. Naturally, such customers and end users will expect that all offerings, regardless of who supplies them, will be able to be used as substitutes for each another. In that way, if one supplying organization has problems with producing or providing an offering, the customer or end user can simply increase purchases from that organization's competitors.

I first saw this principle put into action by customers in the steel industry. Until around 1980, almost all steel was made from virgin raw materials. At each step in the production process, some of the steel ingredients or the steel would be lost due to flaws, corrosion, and mistakes. As a result, two tons of raw materials might whittle down into one ton of finished steel delivered to the customer. The process typically took several weeks. Steel inventories (unless made of stainless steel) also rapidly deteriorated due to rust and corrosion. So it was highly desirable for those who made finished products out of such steel to obtain a fresh supply just before it was needed.

When dealing with commodity steel, that was no problem. Over time, those who made products from steel wanted to save money and to improve their offerings. To do so, many began seeking steel with higher performance characteristics so that thickness and weight could be reduced ... as well as the total price paid for the metal used in making a given product.

Because there were more failures at various stages in making the higher performance metal, the process became longer. In fact, all the steel being produced might be rejected and then the entire production process would have to start over again ... delaying receipt of finished steel by as much as six weeks.

Naturally, customers who made products from such steel were very concerned about avoiding delays. To do so, these customers typically began purchasing steel from more companies, in hopes that a steadier supply of finished steel would be available to them. To succeed with this, the customer had to be able to describe for each potential supplier an exact specification of what ingredients needed to go into the steel and how well as how the resulting steel needed to perform in various usages.

While everyone knew the results a customer or end user wanted, not all steel companies were equal in knowing how to conduct the steel-making process to gain a customer's desired result. If a producer was given the opportunity to continually make such a custom form of steel, it would eventually gain expertise and become more competent. As a result, steel producers would eventually be able to more readily copy one another.

That's the concept behind seeking customers and end users who demand multiple sourcing: Be sure that others who supply the customers and end users obtain opportunities to learn how to provide exactly what you offer that is superior to the standard offerings.

In making this observation, let me note that the most paranoid and sensitive of such customers and end users may go one step further and require collaboration among their suppliers so that each one can learn from the others. In such a case, you could even be required to throw open your operations so that competitors could see and duplicate what you do. Ah! Sounds like a great way to encourage more copying, doesn't it?

You can also go one step further: Encourage customers and end users to demand multiple sources. I ran into this situation once during a competition between Mitchell and Company and another consulting firm. Rather than discourage the potential client from working with our competitor, I spent a lot of time explaining how our two organizations were so different that we weren't actually competitors. I further pointed out that the client company could learn a great deal by working with both organizations. If the two consulting firms provided the same advice, the client could be much more secure in the decision. If we disagreed, the client could interrogate us to find out why and gain more insight into the pros and cons of what to do next.

Although it cost the client more than twice as much as the company had planned to spend, its team went ahead and hired both organizations. Our conclusions turned out to be identical (for vastly different reasons), and the client was well pleased with the results.

Within a few months, an action somewhat similar to the recommendations was taken, and an executive of the client company later told me it was one of the best decisions the organization had ever made.

I gained a lot of useful knowledge from the experience because I now knew that the other organization's methodology, although different, could deliver similar answers to ours. Since the other organization charged a great deal more than we did, I often made this point to potential clients and probably sold some extra business because of describing this experience.

Emboldened by what happened, I approached some competitors to find out how we could combine our services in ways that would provide clients with what neither organization could do by itself. In the process, we each learned a lot about one another that was useful for potentially copying each other's services.

As you think about what new offerings to develop, you can focus on how you might define products or services (or combinations thereof) that would be so much more essential to your customers (such as providing higher value-added cloud-computing storage) that multiple vendors would surely be used (probably in this case by having duplicate clouds in operation by different vendors). Make a virtue out of that potential requirement by designing your offering in such a way that it will be relatively cheap and easy for customers to work simultaneously with at least two suppliers.

In the process, you'll gain an advantage you probably haven't yet thought about: Your competitors will find themselves needing to copy you, making it easier for other competitors to copy them, as well.

I'm sure you see many of the other advantages of this approach for encouraging copying. Your mutual customers and end users will be continually bringing you together to share information, to deal with mutual problems, and to plan for future offerings.

If the offerings stay undifferentiated without improvements, you will find that your industry will soon bog down into continual price wars. Your ability to innovate will be essential to creating more added value for all stakeholders. No one will miss that message, and encouragement to innovate should be unusually high. Notice, too, that innovations will probably spread more rapidly because of having multiple sources, so that the risk for customers and end users will be reduced during each shift into new offerings.

What's the key lesson? *An industry-leading organization that sincerely wants to accelerate its useful innovations can be helped by focusing on customers and end users who demand multiple sourcing.*

Your Lesson Nine Assignments

1. How could you and your stakeholders benefit because your competitors become involved as mutual sources for all of your customers and end users?

2. If competitors become involved as mutual sources to all of your customers and end users, what would have to change about your innovation priorities, budgets, processes, and practices to encourage such competition?

3. How could you use competitors becoming involved as mutual sources for all your customers and end users as an advantage for stimulating your future innovations?

4. What else could you do now to encourage making valuable innovations available much sooner from your organization ... beyond competitors becoming involved as mutual sources to all your customers and end users?

5. How can you prepare in advance to make any gains in increasing competitors' copying by their becoming involved as mutual sources for all your customers and end users even more productive for your organization, your stakeholders, and the industry?

Lesson Ten

Endorse Competitors' Offerings

*Now John was clothed with camel's hair and
with a leather belt around his waist,
and he ate locusts and wild honey.*

*And he preached, saying,
"There comes One after me who is mightier than I,
whose sandal strap I am not worthy
to stoop down and loose.
I indeed baptized you with water, but
He will baptize you with the Holy Spirit."*

— Mark 1:6-8 (NKJV)

In the Bible, God often employed prophets to send messages intended to help pave the way for important future events for His Kingdom. In Mark 1:6-8 (NKJV), we see part of the testimony of John the Baptist describing the future actions of Jesus. While I'm sure John did not see himself as a competitor of Jesus, the Son of God, John's testimony undoubtedly increased the initial acceptance of Jesus when He began teaching.

To the best of my knowledge, businesses seldom benefit from God sending prophets to praise their offerings. However, many businesses find that they can accomplish more if credible people and organizations endorse their offerings. Despite the potential advantages, rarely will a business ask a competitor to do so. Let's look at this opportunity.

What does it mean to endorse a competitor's offering? In most cases, such an action first involves obtaining the offering (which is usually easier to do if it's a product, rather than a service) and testing it for fidelity to its published standards and its effectiveness in providing benefits for customers, end users, and other stakeholders. The actual endorsement may mean that you declare that the offering can be substituted for your offering or used in conjunction with your offering. The most important part of this process is that you make the endorsement public so that anyone can learn about it. Because you are seen as an industry leader due to your innovations, your endorsement will undoubtedly help sales of such a competitor's offering.

Why would you want to endorse a competitor's offering? While there are many potential purposes, in this discussion we focus on encouraging copying of your own organization's offerings.

Why would endorsing a competitor's offering encourage copying of your offerings? Well, an endorsement doesn't unless you intend for your endorsement to have such an effect. Here are seven elements that constitute one way to use an endorsement to encourage such copying:

1. Identify high quality competitive offerings that can be used to substitute for or in conjunction with your offering due to the competitors' offerings being quite similar (i.e., copies) to what you provide.
2. Contact your competitors to see if these organizations would like to receive an endorsement.
3. If a competitor is interested, ask the competitor what kind of endorsement would be most valuable.
4. If possible, supply that kind of an endorsement.
5. Permit your competitor to use the endorsement in its marketing and offering materials.

6. Provide the endorsement to your customers, end users, and stakeholders so that they will feel encouraged by your organization to consider using the competitor offerings that copy what you do.
7. Make it clear that the endorsement is limited to the testing you've done, the competitor's fidelity to what was true at the time of testing, and the status of your own offerings. So, for instance, if you later improve your offering so that the competitor's offering is no longer an effective copy, your endorsement should stop.

As you can easily imagine, if your endorsement has become valuable to a competitor, no grass will grow under its feet in seeking to keep that endorsement. So when you innovate, the competitor will want to copy in ways that help regain the endorsement.

Why would such endorsements encourage your own organization to be more innovative? Most people go into business, in part, because they are fascinated by the idea of making a decision or taking an action and seeing what happens. It's an intriguing prospect. For those who feel this way, the opportunity will be quite interesting to add an innovation that at least some competitors will be in a great rush to copy. Here are three intriguing things to think about:

1. See how much demand forms for your new offering or upgraded version. Remember that no one is likely to be able to match what you do immediately. Seeing large demand develop can be immensely gratifying.
2. Observe how long it takes for competitors to provide decent substitutes that are copies. The longer it takes, the more satisfying it can be to have provided the innovation.
3. Think about competitors scrambling to do what your organization was able to take its time doing.

In an industry where you continually encourage copying, those who are highly competitive in your organization can feel a little stifled. Moments of being able to produce an innovation could seem a bit like an athlete might feel after setting a new world's record. Certainly, the athlete knows that any such sports record will be eventually matched and superseded. But until then, it's certainly gratifying to be so accomplished. The same emotional reaction holds true for many businesspeople.

There will probably be publicity about your innovations in such an environment, the sort of thing that can provide your organization with an opportunity to give recognition to those who did fine work in creating the improvement. Everyone likes to be appreciated, and your organization can use such moments as one way to do so.

People also like to work for an organization that they see as being a winner. Having competitors working hard to gain your approval will reinforce stakeholders' sense that they are winners themselves. As a result, they will be highly supportive of making improvements that reinforce this perception.

I could certainly describe other psychological and practical benefits, but I'm sure you get the idea.

If you doubt how powerful such emotions can be, consider the rivalry between Amazon.com and Barnes & Noble, competitors for online books and music. Amazon.com has tried to gain exclusive access to new electronic products and provided large economic incentives to obtain it. In retaliation, Barnes & Noble announced it would no longer sell books or music published by Amazon.com. Just imagine how that industry would be transformed if, instead, Amazon.com was endorsing Barnes & Noble's electronic reader and paying authors and musicians extra to offer their products through Barnes & Noble, as well as Amazon.com. Is there any doubt that Barnes & Noble would be more cooperative and quickly make its electronic reader a better copy of and functional substitute for the Amazon Kindle?

What's the key lesson? *An industry-leading organization that sincerely wants to accelerate its useful innovations can be helped by endorsing competitors' offerings that are effective copies and substitutes for its own offerings.*

<u>Your Lesson Ten Assignments</u>

1. How could you and your stakeholders benefit because you endorse competitors' offerings that are effective copies and substitutes for your own offerings?

2. If you endorse competitors' offerings that are effective copies and substitutes for your own offerings, what else would have to change about your innovation priorities, budgets, processes, and practices to encourage such a circumstance?

3. How could you use endorsing competitors' offerings that are effective copies and substitutes for your own offerings as an advantage for stimulating your future innovations?

4. What else could you do now to encourage making valuable innovations available much sooner from your organization ... beyond endorsing competitors' offerings that are effective copies and substitutes for your own offerings?

5. How can you prepare in advance to make any gains in increasing competitors' copying from endorsing competitors' offerings that are effective copies and substitutes for your own offerings even more productive for your organization, your stakeholders, and the industry?

Lesson Eleven

Make Improvements That Will Attract A Competitor's Highest Profile Customers

Then Agrippa said to Paul,
"You are permitted to speak for yourself."

So Paul stretched out his hand
and answered for himself:
"I think myself happy, King Agrippa,
because today I shall answer for myself
before you concerning all the things
of which I am accused by the Jews,
especially because you are expert
in all customs and questions
which have to do with the Jews.
Therefore I beg you to hear me patiently."

— Acts 26:1-3 (NKJV)

In Acts 26:1-3 (NKJV), the false imprisonment of the Apostle Paul gave him an opportunity to share his testimony and the Gospel message with King Agrippa, someone whose Salvation could have helped attract new believers. While Paul didn't set out to be imprisoned so that he would have a chance to convert influential people, God used his circumstances for that end, first in the Promised Land and later in Rome. This engagement foreshadows in some ways the ultimate conversion of the Roman emperor Constantine, whose acceptance of Christianity greatly sped growth of the faith.

Similarly, while a high profile customer may only represent a small percentage of industry volume, switching such a customer can be a huge blow to a competitor by causing other customers to rethink their use of the competitor's offerings. In past lessons, we have considered milder ways to attract a competitor's attention, such as by creating an offering advantage that can be persuasively demonstrated in advertising so that no self-respecting competitor would fail to want to improve by copying your innovation, the subject of Lesson Five.

We looked at that alternative because you may sometimes face situations where it makes more sense to "nudge" a competitor to copy rather than to "bulldoze" a copycat reaction. One possible example is where your competitor's unit is smaller than yours, but the unit is part of a much larger organization with substantial resources that could potentially swamp your own organization's capabilities. In such a circumstance, it would be better to "nudge" the competitor to start copying ... rather than to "threaten" the competitor.

How else might such a warning be provided? Rather than attacking the competitors' biggest vulnerability, you might attack a medium-sized vulnerability: adding improvements that will attract purchases from a competitor's highest profile customers.

Who are those customers? Here are five possibilities:

1. Those pictured or listed in the competitor's annual report to shareholders
2. Those pictured or listed in product brochures

3. Those who have appeared with the competitor's personnel in articles published by the industry association
4. A competitor's customers who have presented awards for outstanding performance to the competitor
5. Customers whom everyone in the industry monitors for some reason or another, especially if they are bellwethers of new trends.

I could make a longer list, but I'm sure you have ideas that better relate to your industry.

You can start by surveying as many of your competitor's high profile customers as possible. As part of the survey, find out which of the competitor's other accounts high profile customers pay attention to in evaluating when it's time to make a change in suppliers. Find out also why each one buys from the competitor rather than from your organization. Focus on questions related to all differences between you and the competitor.

From the survey, you should be able to estimate the volume each customer represents. By reverse engineering the competitor's offerings and methods of operating, you should also be able to estimate profit contribution per unit. Combine the apparent volumes with the survey answers for what different characteristics are providing the competitor in volume and profit contribution. Then, pick some aspect or aspects of the competitor's advantages that represent between 5 percent and 8 percent of total profit contribution solely located within high profile accounts. That's the size of advantage that you should consider leapfrogging past to attract some of the high profile customers.

Before fixing on a particular advantage to overcome and to turn into a disadvantage for the competitor, you also need to think about how you can speed the competitor learning that you have taken some or all of the volume from one of its high profile accounts. Ideally, you would like the head of the competitor's operating unit to call on the head of such a customer's organization. In this way, the undiluted information that the competitor has fallen behind will sooner be received and understood.

Such a program can be especially inspirational to your own staff because they will sense an opportunity to accomplish something that they can take some credit for and enjoy talking about. It's a little like the Native American tradition in some tribes of having adolescent boys seek to touch their enemies, rather than to kill them, as a way to earn honor.

If the competitor continues to ignore innovations, you can repeat this kind of nudge from time to time to encourage copying.

What's the key lesson? *An industry-leading organization that sincerely wants to accelerate its useful innovations can be helped by making improvements that can attract some or all of the volume from a competitor's highest profile customers so that the competitor will feel required to copy.*

Your Lesson Eleven Assignments

1. How could you and your stakeholders benefit because you make improvements that can attract some or all of the volume from a competitor's highest profile customers so that the competitor will feel required to copy you?

2. If you make improvements that can attract some or all of the volume from a competitor's highest profile customers so that the competitor will feel required to copy you, what would have to change about your innovation priorities, budgets, processes, and practices to encourage such a circumstance?

3. How could you use making improvements that can attract some or all of the volume from a competitor's highest profile customers so that the competitor will feel required to copy you as an advantage in stimulating your future innovations?

4. What else could you do now to encourage making valuable innovations available much sooner from your organization ... beyond putting in improvements that can attract some or all of the volume from a competitor's highest profile customers so that the competitor will feel required to copy you?

5. How can you prepare in advance to make more innovation gains by increasing competitors' copying due to improvements that can attract some or all of the volume from a competitor's highest profile customers so that the competitor will feel required to copy you?

Lesson Twelve

Make Improvements That Attract Your Competitors' Least Profitable Customers

And it happened when He was in a certain city,
that behold, a man who was full of leprosy saw Jesus;
and he fell on his face and implored Him, saying,
"Lord, if You are willing, You can make me clean."

Then He put out His hand and touched him, saying,
"I am willing; be cleansed."

Immediately the leprosy left him.

— Luke 5:12-13 (NKJV)

During Jesus' ministry, leprosy was considered such an awful condition that lepers had to live apart from other Jews. For instance, they could not even go to the Temple to worship God. They also had to warn everyone else to stay away from them by shouting that they were unclean. Touching them made the person who did so unclean, as well, so that this person was temporarily cut off from being with others. Yet the Old Testament spoke of the Messiah as being the One who would heal leprosy.

In performing such a healing, Jesus was assisting a person considered to be the least desirable in the community and helping him in a way that spoke volumes about who He was.

In business, finding ways to profit from customers who are relatively unappealing to competitors can be a powerful way of demonstrating the effectiveness of your innovative capabilities, as well as of interesting your competitors in copying to gain profitable advantages.

In Lesson Five, we considered a milder way to attract a competitor's attention by simply creating an offering advantage that could be persuasively demonstrated in advertising so that no self-respecting competitor would fail to copy your innovation.

We looked at that alternative because you may sometimes face situations where it makes more sense to "nudge" a competitor into copying rather than to "bulldoze" a copycat reaction. You could choose, instead, to attack a medium-sized vulnerability. In Lesson Eleven, we considered one way: adding improvements that will attract purchases from a competitor's highest profile customers.

In this lesson, we explore still another way to encourage copying through a nudge: Show substantial profit potential where competitors are probably paying little current attention — providing for low profit-margin customers.

Even if your purpose is to increase copying by a specific competitor, there will be times when attacking all competitors will be necessary. That broader approach is most valuable when you want to soften your nudge of a specific competitor so it doesn't kick off a mindless reaction, such as a price war from which no producer or service provider would gain any advantage.

You might think of this method as being a four-carrots-and-one-stick nudge. Let me explain. Even if you took away a considerable number of a competitor's low-profit margin customers, the overall profit impact would probably be small (well less than 10 percent). Seeing that you are likewise succeeding with other competitors in the industry causes each one to see a larger potential reward from copying … if some of the other competitors' customers can be profitably added.

So this action by your organization might be viewed as an opportunity by a competitor to double volume from low-margin customers by regaining some customers who were lost and attracting some new volume from competitors who don't put the improvement in place. Notice that the improvement also makes the low-profit customers more profitable. Copying that approach could be viewed by the competitors as potentially doubling the profit potential of gaining double the prior volume.

The one stick involved in the nudge is, of course, losing a bit of profit from lost low-profit customers due to not copying the innovation.

Naturally, such a copying response can be encouraged by having the improvement be one that's quick, easy, and relatively inexpensive to make.

Well, it's one thing to build such a hypothetical case. I'm sure you are eager to read about a real example of this occurring. Let me describe one that's well documented in the business literature that you may already know.

The traditional strategy for gaining export market share by Japanese companies has been to focus first on the low-price end of the market by providing superior products at lower prices. The best documented examples are in copiers and in vehicles.

However, realize that the Japanese companies had a different intention than I've stated here. They were usually attempting to grab some volume that would cause few, if any, competitive reactions from the market leaders. As a result, Japanese firms made changes that were difficult, expensive, and time-consuming to copy. Typically, such changes involved reducing quality standards in ways that customers didn't care about and investing some of the savings into making quality improvements that customers did care about.

In automobiles, Japanese companies did so by reducing the expected life of all components and materials to just fit the length of time that most people kept their vehicles on the road. Detroit manufacturers had typically overprovided durability in certain components (such as frames) and materials. However, Detroit manufacturers often skimped on things that were visible to customers that they cared about, especially in fit and finish, and made large numbers of initial assembly errors that had to be corrected by a dealer. Successfully making such changes required decades for American manufacturers to learn and the process of mastering them is still incomplete.

In copiers, Japanese manufacturers reduced the size of machines, simplified the machines' operations so that many fewer parts were needed, and emphasized straight-line paper paths. Such machines were less costly to make and assemble, and required many fewer service calls. Here's a case where the improvements weren't terribly difficult to make, and Xerox responded soon enough to be able to retain parts of the copier market.

In many categories of products and services today, the lowest-priced item is not intended to be purchased by anyone. Such an item is just there to serve as an alternative that will make the medium-priced alternative offering more appealing in terms of value. A competitor who wants to encourage copying could, instead, make the lowest-priced item the medium-priced alternative of its line. The competitor can do so by dropping some features and choices that many people don't really need (or don't put much value on) from the current medium-price alternative and adding some new benefits that customers feel strongly about that are not terribly expensive to provide.

Let me give you an example of what this might look like in practice. Gillette has led the shaving market for a century by providing reusable razors that use disposable blades. When those blades are dull, you need new ones. The cost of those blades has gone through the roof as more and more blades were added along with lubricating strips.

Now, those blades aren't usually worn out. Why not sharpen them and add new lubricating strips when needed?

Disposable razors are now the industry's lowest profit-margin item. Someone who wanted to nudge Gillette into copying might create a new system that would permit sharpening the blades on disposable razors and adding new lubricating strips. Such a system might sell for the price of 10 disposable razors and allow them to last five times as long. If you use the system to extend the usefulness of two disposable razors, you've earned your money back from buying the system. I believe that such a piece of equipment would be cheap to make and highly profitable. There would also be ongoing profits from selling lubricating strips or materials for applying lubrication to used disposable razors. If the company making the innovation wasn't previously doing much volume in disposable razors, such a firm would earn a great profit improvement from the innovation. Gillette could probably copy and have its own version of the innovation into the market in weeks. That is the sort of competitive nudge that I have in mind.

If the competitor were to provide, instead, such equipment for Gillette's main disposable razor-blade products, there would be a battle royal. Gillette would have no choice but to use every competitive weapon it could. The fight wouldn't be pretty. However, by copying the disposable razor innovation, Gillette would see itself as effectively discouraging a competitor from extending such an improvement to its disposable blades.

Naturally, your market and your competitors present different issues. If you need help in sorting out what's a good way for you to use this strategy for copying, please let me know.

What's the key lesson? *An industry-leading organization that sincerely wants to accelerate its useful innovations can be helped by making improvements that can attract some or all of the volume from competitors' lowest profit-margin customers at a good profit, so that the target competitor will feel encouraged to copy.*

Your Lesson Twelve Assignments

1. How could you and your stakeholders benefit because you make improvements that can attract some or all of the volume from competitors' lowest profit-margin customers at a good profit, so that the target competitor will feel encouraged to copy you?

2. If you make improvements that can attract some or all of the volume from competitors' lowest profit-margin customers at a good profit so that the target competitor will feel encouraged to copy you, what would have to change about your innovation priorities, budgets, processes, and practices to encourage such a circumstance?

3. How could you use improvements that can attract a competitor's lowest profit-margin customers at a good profit so that the target competitor will feel encouraged to copy you as an advantage in stimulating your future innovations?

4. What else could you do now to encourage making valuable innovations available much sooner from your organization ... beyond making improvements that can attract some or all of the volume from competitors' lowest profit-margin customers at a good profit so that the target competitor will feel encouraged to copy you?

5. How can you prepare in advance to make more innovation gains by increasing competitors' copying from your improvements that can attract some or all of the volume from competitors' lowest profit-margin customers at a good profit so that the target competitor will feel encouraged to copy you?

Lesson Thirteen

Upgrade Offerings in Ways That Make Your Competitors' Offerings Seem Dated

"No one puts a piece of unshrunk cloth
on an old garment;
for the patch pulls away from the garment,
and the tear is made worse.

"Nor do they put new wine into old wineskins,
or else the wineskins break,
the wine is spilled,
and the wineskins are ruined.

"But they put new wine into new wineskins,
and both are preserved."

— Matthew 9:16-17 (NKJV)

In Matthew 9:16-17 (NKJV), Jesus provides part of His answer to John's disciples concerning why His disciples didn't fast, while the Pharisees and John's disciples did: Being with Him is a time to rejoice in a new life, with plenty of fasting to come after He leaves the disciples behind. In doing so, Jesus points out the fundamental incompatibility of combining some old and new things.

From Jesus' observations, we can discern a lesson about how to influence a competitor to be more active in copying: Make customers see a competitor's offerings as being old and dated. In this lesson, we explore this mild form of encouraging competitors to copy. Now is a particularly good time to make such changes, due to the rapid proliferation of new technologies, business models, and ways of serving customers.

I was originally encouraged to discuss this approach in 2011 after hearing a financial commentator talk about how Facebook's business model for mobile devices was hopelessly dated in providing online experiences on a cell phone. Instead, the company needed to build an application from the ground up to maximize what people like to do with cell phones.

Even if your purpose is to gain copying from a specific competitor, there are times when attacking all competitors in identical ways will be necessary. The broader approach is most valuable when you want to make your nudge of a specific competitor still milder, so that it doesn't kick off a mindless and harmful reaction, such as a price war from which few producer or service-provider stakeholders gain any advantage.

You might think of this method as the equivalent of a teenage girl showing up at the prom in a gorgeous new designer gown, knowing that every other girl will be wearing a less expensive, off-the-rack dress. All eyes will be on that girl, at least for one night. While she may lose some girlfriends in the process, I'm sure she won't lack for dating opportunities.

Everyone likes to think of him- or herself as being a leader, as well as being in step with the times. Yet, what was once cutting-edge eventually comes to be seen as dowdy and old-fashioned.

Most companies are slow to update just for the purposes of seeming to be more *au courant*. Being slow to change is one way that they save money. As a consequence, the colors of items may not be in vogue. The designs may be reflective of 20 years earlier rather than the current part of the twenty-first century. Providing service may be based on telephone directories with endless computer menus that waste your time and frustrate you. The electronic presence may be aimed at publishing information, rather than building a community.

In most cases, I suggest that you also add some functional improvements that are unrelated to bringing your offerings up-to-date. In that way, the pressure on competitors to respond by copying will be much greater. Otherwise, some might dismiss what you do as mere "window dressing." It could take a few years of lost sales by a competitor to trigger a copying reaction in such an instance.

How might you execute such a strategy? I believe that surveys of the competitors' largest customers are the key. In addition to asking about functional requirements that competitors aren't providing, ask about how "up-to-date" each of the competitors' offerings, services, and ways of doing business are. Ask their customers what it is that makes them feel that the competitors are or are not "up-to-date."

Naturally, if you find that an area needing improvements where competitors also aren't up-to-date, that's a great place to make your improvements. Such was the situation with Facebook's competitors in considering how poorly that site formerly appeared on mobile devices. If such a combination of opportunities is not the case, look for opportunities where more improvements would always be seen as beneficial and such performance is also seen as a sign of being up-to-date, even though competitors' customers are currently satisfied. An example might involve increasing battery life in mobile devices by another three hours.

If you don't have either of these opportunities, focus on small functional improvements in a number of areas important to competitors' customers where being up-to-date is more often noticed. In doing so, don't neglect the visual, auditory, and touch experiences that can make interaction seem more natural and comfortable.

As you develop improvements, work closely with competitors' customers to be sure that they view what you are going to provide as being improvements and valuable updates. Otherwise, this strategy could backfire by making you more vulnerable to competitors' current offerings and services. You also gain a benefit in doing so by sending an earlier message to the competitors that you are making a move. In this way, you increase the likelihood of earlier copying.

The people in organizations who design and sell offerings like nothing better than being asked to update offerings and related services. Such people usually have been developing lists of what they would change if only there were funds available and a mandate for improvement. By turning them loose, you may even spark some startling improvements that will payoff bigger than you expect if the changes become popular.

What's the key lesson? *An industry-leading organization that sincerely wants to accelerate its useful innovations can be helped by making improvements that cause competitors' offerings to seem so dated that the targeted competitor will feel compelled to copy.*

Your Lesson Thirteen Assignments

1. How could you and your stakeholders benefit because you make improvements that cause competitors' offerings to seem so dated that competitors will feel compelled to copy you?

2. If you put in improvements that make competitors' offerings seem dated so that competitors will feel compelled to copy you, what would have to change about your innovation priorities, budgets, processes, and practices to encourage achieving such a result?

3. How could you use putting in improvements that make competitors' offerings seem dated so that the competitors will feel compelled to copy you as an advantage in stimulating your future innovations?

4. What else could you do now to encourage valuable innovations being available much sooner from your organization ... beyond putting in improvements that make competitors' offerings seem so dated so that competitors will feel compelled to copy you?

5. How can you prepare in advance to make more innovation gains by increasing competitors' copying from putting in improvements that make competitors' offerings seem so dated that competitors will feel compelled to copy you?

Lesson Fourteen

Make It Easy for Competitors To Reverse Engineer Your Improved Offerings

Then Jesus said to them,

"Follow Me, and
I will make you become fishers of men."

— Mark 1:17 (NKJV)

In Mark 1:17 (NKJV), Jesus invites Andrew and Simon, brothers who are fishermen by vocation, to leave their work behind and become fishers of men, an allusion to helping win souls by sharing the Gospel and their witness of what Jesus had done. Jesus also invited others to follow Him, but He seldom made the invitation easy to embrace. For instance, the rich young ruler was told to first sell all of his possessions and to give to the poor.

By Jesus providing the miracle of net-breaking, boat-swamping amounts of fish before making the invitation, He made it easier for Andrew and Simon to choose following Him. Making your improved offerings easier to duplicate through engineering analysis can be a good way to follow His good example in attracting Andrew and Simon.

While in some cases it will be desirable to permit or even encourage cloning your offerings so that competitors can more easily enter the industry and prosper, at other times cloning will neither be attractive nor possible. Stay tuned. I have more to say about cloning in Lesson Thirty-Two. In this lesson, we look, instead, at what to do when clones don't make sense or cannot be easily done, but you would like to accomplish somewhat similar results.

Dictionary.com defines the verb "reverse-engineer" (with an object) as:

> to study or analyze (a device, as a microchip for computers) in order to learn details of design, construction, and operation, perhaps to produce a copy or an improved version.

Think of reverse engineering as the competitor's initial step in fast copying or improving your organization's offering. The other steps needed to move quickly involve spelling out all the processes and techniques used to obtain the results that customers and end users most value.

For a competitor, reverse engineering can avoid going down many blind alleys and making many of the mistakes that are involved in creating an innovation from scratch. Consequently, the copy (or copy-based improvement) is produced at lower cost, takes less time to develop, and has fewer initial flaws.

These are all important benefits because most truly innovative offerings begin with significant flaws and drawbacks. Even today with much-improved quality practices in place, many people will advise buyers to wait for the second model provided by an innovator before purchasing a new kind of offering. After that amount of time, the price will be lower, the flaws will be mostly gone, and important benefits will have been added. The only thing that can't be accomplished by such a "wait and see" approach is gaining the bragging rights and any truly breakthrough benefits of having something new ahead of others.

With a product, such a reverse-engineering investigation usually begins by purchasing the item. From there, the most knowledgeable technical people in the competitor organization disassemble the offering, taking lots of photographs as they do. Each part is investigated to identify what it is made of, what processes were involved in its manufacture, the purposes of the part, and how each part was assembled to work with other parts.

Next, engineers, production experts, cost analysts, and marketing specialists investigate how the offering might be improved in terms of either its benefits or its costs. After that investigation is complete, a decision is made whether to make a copy or an improvement. From there, the specifications of a new competitive offering are finalized and approved. Work then begins on providing the new competitive offering.

What about services? Although the term "reverse engineering" isn't often applied to investigating services, it's clear that a parallel process can certainly be applied. With so many services now heavily dependent on automation, there's a major technology component for providing at least certain aspects of most services that lends itself to such analysis. Because the technology base for many such services isn't able to be purchased and pulled apart in a laboratory, the investigation may, instead, relate more to measuring performance of a service as a clue to determining how the service is provided in terms of equipment, software, and human involvement.

Notice that although reverse engineering is pretty quick for investigating many products, it's far from being something that can be done in just a few days. If you want to encourage copying, one objective should be to reduce the time and cost of doing such reverse engineering.

Let's look first at some ways such time and cost reductions might be made available for products. Here are six suggestions:

1. Use parts that are commonly available from well-known suppliers that can be easily identified as such.

2. Give suppliers permission to reveal to competitors the parts you use in your offerings.
3. Add descriptions and directions to the offering that spell out more details about the infrastructure for, construction of, and workings of the offering.
4. Avoid proprietary solutions as much as possible, especially in software and other aspects of providing the offering that may be largely invisible to a current or potential competitor.
5. Purchase any new types of parts or software from vendors who insist on providing the same to your competitors.
6. Label as many aspects of the offering as possible to help identify who the suppliers are.

While providing such aids to reverse engineering for a product or even a service, it's also good to consider how easy it will be for competitors to begin producing a similar or improved version. Here are seven examples of appropriate things to consider:

1. Use suppliers who will have enough capacity to take on the added volume that competitors will probably be purchasing.
2. Select suppliers who will be interested in handling the kinds of initial volumes competitors will need.
3. Try to work with suppliers who sell their offerings for similar prices to all comers so that your competitors will not have discouraging cost disadvantages while copying or trying to improve on your offering.
4. Avoid production, provision, and service processes that are hard to learn and to practice.
5. Choose designs that are likely to work well if substantial changes are made either for reasons of cosmetic appeal or for adding other features.
6. Make fixing defective offerings easy and inexpensive to do.
7. Make it easier for your offering to work effectively in conjunction with a potential copy or improvement from a com-

petitor, so that your customers won't be discouraged from purchasing from a new competitor.

If you make it that easy to copy you, what's to keep your competitors from simply taking the market away from you? Well, it's not as though your offering will come out on a Monday and the competitor will beat it on Tuesday. In most cases, the time from seeing or using your new offering to the first occasion when a competing offering can be purchased will be at least a year. If the offering lifecycles are shorter than that, you have nothing at all to fear with many customers. It's usually only if it will be longer than two years before you bring out an improved version that you should have some concerns about how easy you make it to reverse engineer, copy, and improve on what you provide. If competitors will follow much faster than in a year, adjust your analysis of how much lead time you need accordingly and make it harder to reverse engineer and copy your offerings.

If your lifecycle for an offering is considerably longer than two years, you can also arrange to make it more appealing for customers to buy what you provide within the first two years the new offering is out to create additional competitive insulation. Doing so is a great idea because your actions will make competitors especially eager to find ways to get to market sooner.

Knowing that competitors will be predictably coming along with lower prices and/or more benefits will keep your most innovative people stirred to find something better to provide. If they aren't stirred enough, the marketing staff and salespeople will encourage that feeling by talking up what they see as the approaching wave of competition.

What's the key lesson? *An industry-leading organization that sincerely wants to accelerate its useful innovations can be helped by making it easier for existing and new competitors to reverse engineer its offerings and to reach market faster with copies and improvements.*

Your Lesson Fourteen Assignments

1. How could you and your stakeholders benefit because you make it easier for existing and new competitors to reverse engineer your offerings and to reach market faster with copies and improvements?

2. If you make it easier for existing and new competitors to reverse engineer your offerings and to reach market faster with copies and improvements, what would have to change about your innovation priorities, budgets, processes, and practices to encourage such a circumstance?

3. How could you use making it easier for existing and new competitors to reverse engineer your offerings and to reach market faster with copies and improvements as an advantage in stimulating your future innovations?

4. What else could you do now to encourage valuable innovations being available much sooner from your organization ... beyond making it easier for existing and new competitors to reverse engineer your offerings and to reach market faster with copies and improvements?

5. How can you prepare in advance to make any gains in increasing competitors' and accelerating reverse engineering of your new offerings so that competitors' copies and improvements reach market faster even more productive for your organization, your stakeholders, and the industry?

Lesson Fifteen

Leave Gaps in Offering Features That Competitors Can Easily Fill

"Stand before God for the people,
so that you may bring the difficulties to God.
And you shall teach them
the statutes and the laws, and
show them the way in which they must walk
and the work they must do.
Moreover you shall select
from all the people able men,
such as fear God, men of truth,
hating covetousness; and
place such over them to be rulers of thousands,
rulers of hundreds, rulers of fifties,
and rulers of tens.

"And let them judge the people at all times.
Then it will be that every great matter
they shall bring to you, but
every small matter they themselves shall judge.

"So it will be easier for you,
for they will bear the burden with you."

— Exodus 18:19-22 (NKJV)

In Exodus 18:19-22 (NKJV), Moses' father-in-law, Jethro, offers advice about how Moses can better handle the responsibilities of leading the Israelites and judging their disputes. Jethro's solution is to delegate the less important work to others who are well able to handle it. As the Bible reminds us, no one has all the spiritual gifts. We accomplish more of what God intends by combining our gifts in righteous ways.

In business, we can similarly look to leaving tasks for competitors to do in copying or improving on our offerings that would be a distraction for us from our main purpose of expanding innovation so that many more stakeholder benefits are produced. When such a division of focus occurs, all benefit.

Steve Jobs, by Walter Isaacson, was again a resource for this lesson. When Amazon.com launched the Kindle Fire, a lower-priced version of the iPad that provided fewer features based on the Google Android operating system, many criticized the Fire. Some people who considered buying the Kindle Fire were surprised to find that it did not use the latest version of Android, but, rather, employed one that was two releases out-of-date. In addition, the initial device didn't permit downloading a newer version of Android. However, upgrades to Amazon.com's own software were almost immediately available.

As I thought about these initial product characteristics, my conclusion was that Amazon.com decided that having a reading device that could also serve in some ways as a tablet computer would be a hot item at Christmas, and that giving it a low price point was essential to success.

Amazon.com reportedly sold the Kindle Fire at a price that was less than its combined component and manufacturing costs. Clearly, earning profits depended on selling electronic copies of books, videos, movies, games, and software. As long as these content-acquiring functions were working just fine, it didn't matter all that much if the device wasn't as good as it might have been for e-mail and other interactive applications of mobile computing.

Providing more functionality would have taken more time and added costs. In that case, fewer Kindle Fires would have been sold in the first twelve months after the actual launch due to the product having been delayed, and the price would have been higher. Overall profits for Amazon.com would certainly have been lower in the quarter when the Kindle Fire was launched.

As I pondered what looked like a good business decision, it occurred to me that Amazon.com's decision might have also been supported in part by a different logic. Let me explain what occurred to me.

Many people expected that an iPad 3 would become available in the following year, and that this Apple device would probably be thinner, have a better HD touch screen, contain a more powerful microprocessor, feature a better camera, and provide wireless battery charging.

Such a "loaded with features" device from Apple would probably be priced high, likely over $500. The Kindle Fire at $199 was made good enough to be worth upgrading to from a low-end Kindle reader that sold for $79 to $99. The next Kindle release could then be a similar degree of upgrade opportunity for those who loved the Fires, perhaps to one costing $199 to $299 with about half the features of the iPad 3.

Due to its distribution clout and strong relationship with customers, in order to succeed Amazon.com didn't have to be the first to bring out a feature on the Kindle Fire. Amazon.com could watch to see what features competitors would add to their more limited alternatives to the iPad 2 and 3 and then use the lessons of their successes and failures to choose what to add to future upgrades of the Kindle Fire. With the Consumer Electronics Show scheduled just a few weeks later, Amazon.com wouldn't have had to wait long to see announcements from Apple and its own competitive copiers and to start learning how experts and customers responded.

Notice that a strategy of attacking a high-end competitor with a lower-priced, lesser-featured device makes it logical to leave major gaps in offering features that copying competitors can exploit. Did Amazon.com do this on purpose? Perhaps we'll never know, but the effect is the same — regardless of what the original intent was — pointing the way to a superior strategy for encouraging copying that your organization can exploit.

To engage in this strategy, an organization needs the capability of rapidly adding new features to its offerings on short notice. Presumably, this capability might mean applying the latest market intelligence about what the high-end competitor is planning to direct a company's own preliminary design and manufacturing work for adding potential features to the next product release.

What is needed for such a strategy to succeed?

- A clear sense of what offering features might be desirable based on either extensive customer and user research and testing, or the ability to measure how existing offerings with such features are doing in the marketplace
- An opportunity to earn large profits from selling related offerings that don't much depend on the omitted features of the offering that copying competitors can provide
- Nimble design and manufacturing capabilities to add features rapidly and inexpensively whenever needed to stimulate demand for an offering or its own related offerings
- Customer and user relationships that permit some delays in making highly desirable features available in exchange for a much lower price for the current offering

What's the key lesson? *An industry-leading organization that sincerely wants to accelerate its useful innovations can be helped by omitting many potential features that competitors will probably include when they copy a low-end offering, providing rapid, inexpensive insights into how to expand the market and create opportunities for all stakeholders to benefit from that expansion.*

Your Lesson Fifteen Assignments

1. How could you and your stakeholders benefit because your competitors can quickly and easily copy your innovations while adding other features for which there may be high demand, but that will raise the price, in order to assess the market-expansion opportunity?

2. If competitors become more effective copiers of your offerings and adders of potentially attractive features that you deliberately omit, what would have to change about your innovation priorities, budgets, processes, and practices?

3. How could you use leaving out potentially attractive features from your offerings as an advantage in stimulating your future innovations?

4. What else could you do now to encourage making valuable innovations available much sooner from your organization ... beyond leaving out potentially attractive, but expensive, features from your latest offerings?

5. How can you prepare in advance to make any gains in increasing competitors' copying by leaving out potentially attractive features from your latest offerings even more productive for your organization, your stakeholders, and the industry?

Lesson Sixteen

Publicize Flaws in Competitors' Plans That Do Not Involve Copying Your Offerings

When He had called the multitude to Himself,
He said to them,

"Hear and understand:
Not what goes into the mouth
defiles a man; but
what comes out of the mouth,
this defiles a man."

Then His disciples came and said to Him,
"Do You know that the Pharisees were offended
when they heard this saying?"

But He answered and said,
"Every plant which
My heavenly Father has not planted
will be uprooted. Let them alone.
They are blind leaders of the blind.
And if the blind leads the blind,
both will fall into a ditch."

— Matthew 15:10-14 (NKJV)

Jesus had little use for those who said one thing and did another, especially when they claimed to be following God. In Matthew 15 (NKJV), Jesus rebukes the Pharisees in such a way to their faces and then teaches His followers what they should do, instead. In these two actions, Jesus made it possible for the Pharisees to hear what they were doing wrong and for others to learn not to emulate their hypocrisy.

Similarly, criticizing competitors that are not copying can be used to inform them that they should be doing so, as well as warning their stakeholders of potential lost benefits and harm. We'll look at this situation through considering Google and Microsoft.

Google was originally dependent on its search-engine business to sell click-based advertising (advertisers only pay if someone clicks on a button to be redirected to a Web page). Although Google has engaged in other activities, profits were initially limited in the newer areas. Microsoft was similarly dependent on its Windows operating system for personal computers (PCs), which allowed the company to profitably sell its application software in bundles to those who used Windows.

Since the iPad and iPhone were introduced, PC sales have been weak. Google anticipated such a shift occurring and developed its Android operating system for cellular telephones, which became the dominant technology in North America. Microsoft, by comparison, became a minor player in mobile operating systems, compounded by Apple providing the iCloud capability for storage of applications and their contents to those who use iPhones and iPads.

Google's Executive Chairman, Eric Schmidt, at one point commented that Microsoft was caught in a difficult product transition as its traditional PC-based business declined while being a distant also-ran in the newer technologies for mobile communications and computing. At the time, this characterization of Microsoft's circumstances was definitely correct. Why do you suppose Mr. Schmidt made it a point to highlight the circumstance?

Since Mr. Schmidt didn't share his motives with anyone outside of Google, I can only speculate. My guess is that Mr. Schmidt wanted to encourage Microsoft to either copy the Android software in the future or to support this software platform.

Why might such publicity trigger a changed direction by Microsoft? Well, Microsoft long held an advantage in software development by being able to obtain its pick of the best code writers for its staff. In addition, independent developers loved to create applications that fit best with Microsoft's operating systems. Both advantages had substantially eroded.

At the time, many developers preferred to be involved with Apple or Goggle. In this competition, Google had problems staying competitive. Microsoft was the main organization that could strengthen Google's Android platform that hadn't yet done much in this regard.

Mr. Schmidt could also have been sending a message not so much to Microsoft, as to its software developers, making clearer to them that Microsoft will either have to join the Android alliance at some point or copy the alliance's offerings to such a substantial extent that Microsoft might as well be part of the alliance. Either move by Microsoft could be decisive in allowing Google to garner the lion's share of software-development talent for its Android platform and applications. With mobile communications and computing emerging as the dominant platforms for both business and personal use, such an advantage could be decisive against Apple, especially now that Steve Jobs was no longer heading Apple.

Why does publicity become an important tool in this kind of an environment?

First, publicity broadens awareness that a competitor is having problems. That's important because some of the people who should be concerned aren't yet. For instance, a software developer's spouse might ask her or his spouse about what Mr. Schmidt had to say.

Second, such comments also lead people to ask questions who are in a position to force a competitor to respond. Major companies then depended on Microsoft in their offices and on Google outside of their offices for their computing and communications. Many company leaders hadn't yet focused on this split because of not yet addressing such technology compatibility. Such leaders often do spend time, however, with their own heads of Information Technology, and you could expect that there would be pointed questions at some point about the dependability of the firm's computing and communications.

Third, leaders of competitive companies can begin to fear for their jobs and careers due to increased sensitivity of shareholders to the companies not having invested in being copiers or users of a given technology. Such fear can lead to knee-jerk acceptance of copying, either by current leaders or by those who replace them.

Fourth, such comments can cause a reaction among those who haven't been thinking about the implications of copying or not doing so. For instance, I've been in the Windows world for a long time ... despite not especially liking the software. At some point, I'm going to have to make a decision about what sort of computing The 400 Year Project should rely on during global implementation. Due to this comment by Mr. Schmidt, it's clear that I should be thinking about moving out of the Microsoft world. If I do leave, I'm unlikely to return. Although I'm hardly a big technology buyer, comments made on behalf of The 400 Year Project and the technical links provided by the project could easily influence tens of millions of people to move one way or the other in the future.

Notice, too, that there's little risk in publicizing such flaws, just as long as an organization is truthful and doesn't seek to cause harm for harm's sake. Any independent validation of the publicized points by experts and journalists would simply increase and spread an accurate message's impact.

So what should you be doing? I see the following eight steps as important:

1. Determine which of your competitors are most vulnerable to harm when awareness increases of their disadvantages due to not copying what you are doing.

2. Seek to persuade such competitors to start copying through any private communications that are legally allowed.

3. If discussions aren't legally possible or aren't fruitful, consider which messages in what forums would create the most incentive for the most vulnerable competitors to begin copying your offerings.

4. Test your ideas with a single public message to see how well the points are appreciated and how the competitors respond.

5. Give your competitors time to think about the communication and how to respond. This delay should in most cases be at least 60 days.

6. If the communication doesn't obtain the results you want in an appropriate time but the message is definitely influencing key parties, start repeating the communication with additional evidence and in more forums. In doing so, be sympathetic to the competitors in what you say in public ... so you don't start a vendetta with them that can come back to create problems for your own organization or you personally.

7. Wait for a response from the competitor before launching a second major round of broad communications.

8. If at some point the competitor doesn't decide to copy, you should stop this strategy before it becomes irritating to your stakeholders.

What's the key lesson? *An industry-leading organization that sincerely wants to accelerate its useful innovations can be helped by publicizing flaws in competitors' plans due to not copying the leader's offerings after making it easy to do so.*

Your Lesson Sixteen Assignments

1. How could you and your stakeholders benefit because your competitors who do not plan to copy your innovative offerings suddenly become active in doing so?

2. If public knowledge increases about competitors' flawed plans for not copying your innovative offerings, what would have to change about your innovation priorities, budgets, processes, and practices to encourage such copying to begin?

3. How could you use publicizing competitors' flawed plans for not copying your innovative offerings as an advantage in stimulating your future innovations?

4. What else could you do now to encourage making valuable innovations available much sooner from your organization ... beyond publicizing competitors' flawed plans for not copying your innovative offerings?

5. How can you prepare in advance to make any gains in increasing competitors' copying by publicizing competitors' flawed plans for not copying your innovative offerings even more productive for your organization, your stakeholders, and the industry?

Lesson Seventeen

Innovate to Outperform Competitors' Best Features

Then He went into the temple and
began to drive out those
who bought and sold in it, saying to them,

"It is written, 'My house is a house of prayer,'
but you have made it a 'den of thieves.'"

And He was teaching daily in the temple.
But the chief priests, the scribes, and
the leaders of the people sought to destroy Him,
and were unable to do anything;
for all the people
were very attentive to hear Him.

— Luke 19:45-49 (NKJV)

In Jesus' time on Earth, religious leaders held sway over the Temple in Jerusalem. While much of Jesus' ministry occurred in the countryside far from Jerusalem, toward the end of His ministry He was in the Temple challenging the practices there, from the ways that people were profiting from the Temple to the false teachings that were being presented there. In doing so, Jesus undermined the ultimate authority that such leaders had over the Israelites.

In business, some competitors won't take the hint and start innovating to improve on or to copy the innovations you've made accessible to them and their stakeholders. In such cases, at some point you have to directly attack the competitors.

In prior lessons, we discuss various ways of using innovation itself as a method for encouraging copying by your competitors, such as by increasing the frequency of innovation, leaving gaps in your offering line competitors can exploit, and making breakthroughs that you allow competitors to copy. In this lesson, we look, instead, at what to do when such "friendly" ways of encouraging competitive copying aren't producing enough results. Our focus is on how to deliver innovations that will strongly affect any competitor who doesn't immediately copy or improve upon what you provide.

Imagine that you make the world's fastest and most effective software for sniffing out and stopping virus attacks on computers. For years, you've taught everyone who buys such software how fast your software is and how many more threats it can diagnose and stop in less time than can the software of other firms.

Then one morning you turn on television to hear that a well-respected competitor with excellent software for sniffing out and stopping virus attacks has just provided a new offering that's twice as fast as yours ... and even more effective than yours in identifying and stopping such attacks.

Your first reaction is disbelief. You call in your staff to check out the new offering, expecting to learn that it's all "vaporware" (a promise of a new offering that's not yet available in software you can purchase). Instead, your technical team uses its standard methods to evaluate the software and verifies that, if anything, the software works even better than its claims and is certainly available.

After you pick yourself up off the floor, your next action is likely to be ordering your organization to pull out all the stops to produce a still faster and more effective version that will leave the new competitive offering trailing far behind in performance. And you'll probably set a quite short timeline to do so. The race is now on to innovate ... and then, hopefully, to thrive after succeeding with the improvements.

But you are bound to be worried about losing massive numbers of customers in the meantime. What else can you do? Well, you can ask your staff to tear apart the new competitive offering (as we discussed in Lesson Fourteen concerning reverse engineering) and put together a copy that might last in the market until your truly innovative improvements are available, assuming the innovative competitor isn't too aggressive in stopping you with legal actions.

If your competitor's goal is to stir up some innovation and copying competition, glee will shine forth from the competitor's corporate headquarters as the news of your reaction eventually leaks.

Most organizations are led by highly competitive individuals who take any action aimed at offsetting their main advantages as seriously as they take a challenge to their personal honor. If you focus on taking away those advantages through innovation, you are almost certain to foment a faster rate of innovation and copying in these dimensions.

In addition, some executives feel so affronted by such competitive attacks that they will, if affordable, also start working on innovations that will lead to attacking their competitor's foundational advantages with still other innovations. In such an instance, copying will at least double.

Consider, too, that such an increased level of competition will cause other competitors to become much more active in their copying ... or their viability will also be in question.

So how do you create such reactions?

Start by understanding competitors' offerings advantages that account for a very high percentage of the decisions to buy from them, rather than from your organization. You can use customer interviews or surveys to learn that information. Keep it simple so that whatever you learn, your competitor is also likely to pick up in any market research it does, as well, no matter how primitive or poorly done.

If this research and evaluation had been done concerning iPads, there would probably have been many reactions about being "cool," the shape of the tablet computer, the appearance of the icons on the screen, the ease of use, battery life, and so forth. Clearly, the aspect that would hurt Apple the most is any innovation by a competitor that made Apple's offerings "uncool."

Since many people have or will soon have quite good tablet computers in terms of the standard features, it would seem most apparent that what competitors lack are design advantages that would make the iPad look dated. Since design is an area where competitive improvements are always possible, an Apple competitor could hire a number of the world's leading designers to work on the shape, appearance, feel, look, and on-screen appearance of its tablet computers. If tied up under exclusive deals, Apple wouldn't have the option to access those same design resources. Rather than just have one type of tablet computer, the competitor could offer a variety that are perceived as being much more "cool" by the biggest purchasers of such items for a given use. For instance, I'm sure that those who use a tablet computer for portable video watching at home would be looking for different features in appearance and shape than those who use them for work while traveling.

You, too, should seek the optimal combination of purchase-shifting benefits, as well as the ease with which you can innovate in an area to decide what kind of direct innovative attack to make. As you make your improvements, be prepared for counterattacks in the same area of advantage ... as well as in those areas where you currently have advantages. Then, you will be able to make timely responses to whatever the competitor comes back with that will escalate the competitive innovation battle.

Have a great time as you do! This can be a lot of fun. Stakeholders will cheer!

What's the key lesson? *An industry-leading organization that sincerely wants to accelerate its useful innovations can be helped by making it all but impossible for existing competitors to ignore its innovations by*

Advanced Business for Innovation*

providing superior benefits that customers care a lot about in the competitors' key areas of strength.

Your Lesson Seventeen Assignments

1. How could you and your stakeholders benefit because you make it all but impossible for existing competitors to ignore your innovations by providing superior benefits that customers care a lot about in the competitors' key areas of strength?

2. If you make it all but impossible for existing competitors to ignore your innovations by providing superior benefits that customers care a lot about in the competitors' key areas of strength, what would have to change about your innovation priorities, budgets, processes, and practices to encourage such a circumstance?

3. How could you use making it all but impossible for competitors to ignore your innovations by providing superior benefits customers care a lot about in the competitors' key areas of strength as an advantage in stimulating your innovations?

4. What else could you do now to encourage your organization to develop valuable innovations much sooner ... beyond making it all but impossible for existing competitors to ignore your innovations by providing superior benefits that customers care a lot about in the competitors' key areas of strength?

5. How can you prepare in advance to make any gains in increasing competitors' copying by providing superior benefits that customers care a lot about in the competitors' key areas of strength even more productive for your organization, your stakeholders, and the industry?

Lesson Eighteen

Innovate to Gain Highly Admired Bragging Rights

I have fought the good fight,
I have finished the race,
I have kept the faith.

Finally, there is laid up for me
the crown of righteousness,
which the Lord, the righteous Judge,
will give to me on that Day,
and not to me only
but also to all
who have loved His appearing.

— 2 Timothy 4:7-8 (NKJV)

The Apostle Paul brought new meaning to the expression "going beyond the call of duty." Having been a Pharisee who persecuted Christians until Jesus appeared to him, Paul then did whatever it took to share the Gospel message throughout the Jewish and Gentile worlds. In these two sentences written to Timothy, Paul summed up the credit that his faithfulness had brought him in God's eyes.

While Paul did so to please and honor God, in business many people will seek after bragging rights as though such distinctions were a substitute for God's approval. We should be sure not to fall into this trap, but use any bragging rights incidentally acquired, instead, to advance God's Kingdom so that more Godly benefits are provided to more beneficiaries.

I was very surprised the first time I ran into industry bragging rights in aerospace. The executives of a major defense supplier wistfully described to me how their colleagues in other companies had once spoken to them at a club they all belonged to after their company had succeeded in a major space mission. Every person in the company described this recognition as the high point of his or her career ... by a wide margin.

The second time it happened, I wasn't as surprised ... but I still took special note. I was in Detroit visiting one of the three major auto makers. When I mentioned that a competitor had been faltering, the executives I was meeting with pointedly disagreed that there was anything wrong at the other company. As proof, these gentlemen pointed out that the other firm had just seen one of its vehicles selected as the *Motor Trend* Car of the Year.

In response, I didn't have the heart to point out that it didn't matter how many awards the other company won or how many cars of this type it sold, the company wasn't going to prosper. I held back because I could see how envious the executives were that the competitor had gained this honor.

Since then, whenever I first meet an executive, I gently inquire about what accomplishment would mean the most to her or him and the person's firm. After a brief pause, the person will noticeably swallow and describe something that I've probably never heard of. In most cases, it's something like the industry equivalent of a nation's soccer team winning the World Cup.

People want to be on winning teams, and they often associate their own organizations with being "their" team. At the same time, they don't want to be on a losing team. If a firm is always an also-ran in bragging rights (accomplishments that bring enough pride that people want to talk about what has happened), the people feel like also-rans, as well.

In innovation, certain standards are important. The other standards don't provide nearly as much opportunity. For instance, when it comes to missiles, American generals at one time liked them to leave the launch pad very rapidly. If the missiles weren't totally reliable as they did, it didn't matter as much. It was considered more important to have a deterrent that Soviet bombers and missiles couldn't affect.

You can also think about this perspective in terms of the arguments that school children often have. When two boys are disputing, they will often verbally compare one another's size and strength. If one of the youngsters is obviously losing in this comparison, a tried-and-true tactic is to argue that the youngster's father or brother is much bigger than the other youngster's father or brother. The implication is that the physically disfavored child is able to call on the other family member for help in a scuffle or stare down.

So what happens when you choose to innovate in ways that gain such industry bragging rights? The competitors notice and pay attention. They are also likely to redirect a lot of their resources towards trying to outdo what you have just accomplished and been recognized for in this regard in hopes of becoming "top dog" in bragging rights.

In making this suggestion, I also encourage you to engage in this strategy only if the ways to gain such bragging rights add significant value to customers, end users, and other stakeholders, rather than just exciting some group of judges or so-called experts.

You'll also find that seeking to gain bragging rights will be a motivating factor for many people in your organization. It's a way for them to gain recognition beyond the four walls of where they work, adding credibility within and without your organization. Those who win awards in such efforts will also be much sought after by at least some competitors. When that happens, you can count on some of them leaving. And that's good for increasing copying in the industry.

Let's assume you've now won the bragging rights. Your staff isn't going to want to lose them, are they? They will probably redouble their efforts to top what they just accomplished in order to win the next year's recognition. And the more often they succeed, the more determined competitors will be to copy and to improve upon what they did.

I also suspect that you'll have a lot of fun with this strategy. When will you start?

What's the key lesson? *An industry-leading organization that sincerely wants to accelerate its useful innovations can be helped by seeking to gain highly admired bragging rights in ways that customers, end users, and other stakeholders care about.*

Your Lesson Eighteen Assignments

1. How could you and your stakeholders benefit because you seek to gain highly admired bragging rights in ways that customers, end users, and other stakeholders care about?

2. If you seek to gain highly admired bragging rights in ways that customers, end users, and other stakeholders care about, what would have to change about your innovation priorities, budgets, processes, and practices to encourage such a circumstance?

3. How could you use seeking to gain highly admired bragging rights in ways that customers, end users, and other stakeholders care about as an advantage in stimulating your future innovations?

4. What else could you do now to encourage making valuable innovations available much sooner from your organization ... beyond seeking to gain highly admired bragging rights in ways that customers, end users, and other stakeholders care about?

5. How can you prepare in advance to make any gains in increasing competitors' copying from seeking to gain highly admired

bragging rights in ways that customers, end users, and other stakeholders care about even more productive for your organization, your stakeholders, and the industry?

Lesson Nineteen

Publish Your Innovation Methods and Plans

"Go therefore and make disciples of all the nations,
baptizing them in the name of the Father
and of the Son and of the Holy Spirit,
teaching them to observe all things
that I have commanded you; and lo,
I am with you always,
even to the end of the age."

— Matthew 28:19-20 (NKJV)

Throughout the Bible, God has been generous in telling us what to expect. Despite His thoughtfulness, people have long been ignoring His promises and warnings. In Matthew 28:19-20 (NKJV), we see an example in God's plan for creating healthy relationships with His children. Just consider, however, how few people act on these plans and directions each day. Don't be like that!

In business, people can be even more obtuse about identifying what they need to do. Unless you take them by the hand, they may never realize that they are operating in faulty ways.

Consequently, some companies encourage competitive copying by making their own plans and methods more transparent to those who are outside of their own organizations. A company can simply publish the details of its innovation process, the methods used in the process, and what its plans and budgets are.

Naturally, unless your organization is a very large and influential one, chances are that the daily newspaper where you live won't be interested. But you can always put the information on a Web site for your company or in a blog that follows your industry, or send the information to stakeholders ... some of whom are bound to share what you wrote with competitors.

What sort of information should you share? The answer depends a great deal on how much lead time you want to have before competitors respond.

Let's consider a circumstance where your organization is no better (and potentially a lot worse) than competitors in developing market insights. If you immediately release whatever information you have recently gathered from current and potential customers, you run the risk that you may grant a competitor the innovation lead rather than encourage copying. That's too big of a risk to take when just starting to encourage competitors to copy you.

I suggest, instead, that if the development time for bringing an offering to market is at least a year, you allow enough of a time lag in releasing this market information so that your new offerings and improved methods will make it into the market at least a year ahead of any competitors that copy what you provide. If the development time for an offering is less than a year, adjust the delay time for releasing the market insights accordingly to give yourself the most time possible (up to at least a year) for taking your innovative offering and methods to the market first.

Whenever you release such information concerning market insights, a good approach is to stick to big-picture themes and trends. For instance, if consumers want more convenience in the form of reduced time spent on making and cleaning up from meals, share the insight that they want to reduce preparation time (because that's always been true) ... but don't share if they mostly want to save on clean-up time (something that's becoming much more important).

If you want to stimulate a race to make innovations on a regular timetable, then it will be good to start forecasting the rate at which major trends will develop. The semiconductor industry has done such forecasting successfully to encourage copying by predicting when the next generation of chips will be ready to go and what capabilities will be present in those chips. If you learn that by accelerating the rate of introducing new waves of innovation you can accelerate market growth, such forecasts will be especially important. If your organization identifies a good historical correlation between new generations of offerings and growth in demand, publish that.

In almost all cases, anything you can do to shorten the time needed to define new offerings and to bring them to market will naturally be a good strategy for encouraging copying. You should continually measure how long it takes your competitors to copy compared to how long it is taking your organization to innovate.

If you find that your speed of innovation is accelerating versus competitors' copying, one way to help them catch up is by announcing your new products long before they are ready to be provided. Such announcements can help competitors to define new offerings and begin development of them.

If competitors continue to lag in how long it takes for them to copy, consider releasing the details of your new product development process to make it easier for them to streamline their activities along the lines of what you do.

If sharing your development process isn't enough to help competitors speed up, also write about what equipment you use, the best methods for using such equipment, and the fastest ways to train people to more effectively use the equipment.

In other cases, you may have a suspicion that competitors are spending too little time and money on copying what you do. In such circumstances, you can help the development people in competitor organizations to gain more resources by documenting your organization's size, budget, productivity, and contributions to earnings from various innovation activities.

If you discover that some major new technology has to be learned and applied, you will encourage copying by publishing the basis for your conclusions about the technology and what your plans are about a year after you start in this new direction. If you need to acquire certain equipment to do so, give the equipment vendor a generous endorsement. Chances are that such a supplier's sales force will later share that endorsement with your competitors in hopes of making more sales.

What's the key lesson? *An industry-leading organization that sincerely wants to accelerate useful innovation can be helped by publishing its innovation methods and plans so that competitors will focus more resources on faster and more effective copying of the leader's most successful innovations ... thus setting the bar higher for what the leading organization will need to seek to accomplish for itself in innovation.*

Your Lesson Nineteen Assignments

1. How could you and your stakeholders benefit because you publish your innovation methods and plans?

2. What would have to change about your innovation practices if competitors become more effective innovators due to your organization publishing its innovation methods and plans?

3. How could you use publishing your innovation methods and plans to improve your own valuable innovations?

4. What could you do now to encourage making valuable innovations available sooner ... before considering the spur of such enhanced competitors more quickly following in your tracks?

5. How can you prepare in advance to make any gains from publishing your innovation methods and plans even more productive for your organization, your stakeholders, and the industry?

Lesson Twenty

Acquire Dominant Industry Suppliers

Now an angel of the Lord
spoke to Philip, saying,
"Arise and go toward
the south along the road
which goes down from
Jerusalem to Gaza."
This is desert.

So he arose and went.
And behold, a man of Ethiopia,
a eunuch of great authority
under Candace the
queen of the Ethiopians,
who had charge of all her treasury,
and had come to Jerusalem
to worship, was returning.
And sitting in his chariot,
he was reading Isaiah the prophet.

Then the Spirit said to Philip,
"Go near and overtake this chariot."

So Philip ran to him,
and heard him
reading the prophet Isaiah,
and said,
"Do you understand what
you are reading?"

And he said, "How can I,
unless someone guides me?"

— Acts 8:26-31 (NKJV)

In this excerpt from Acts 8 (NKJV), we see the Holy Spirit directing Philip to share the Gospel with a stranger who had great influence in the court of the Ethiopians. The eunuch soon understood the Gospel message and asked Philip to baptize him. According to church lore, this single Salvation was the beginning of many Ethiopians coming to Christ over the ensuing centuries. Similarly, in business having access to a key source of influence can make a great difference in stimulating innovation and competitor copying.

One great way to improve market development is by creating a common base of technology. That approach is especially important in industries where innovation is going to be significant. No customer wants to take a chance on building a business based on the output of a single supplier. If several others can supply what you do, demand will greatly grow.

In many cases, there either are no competitors to work with in establishing an industry standard or there is little interest among credible firms in entering a nascent industry. In such instances, the innovating firm will have to take the lead in establishing a preferred way to provide offerings that serve all stakeholders well.

You can accelerate such a common evolution by acquiring dominant industry suppliers. Naturally, engaging in this opportunity requires that the value of such suppliers be relatively inexpensive compared to the equity value of your firm.

If that relative valuation is not in your favor, also consider approaching the dominant suppliers about the possibility of purchasing just the portion of their organizations and operations that fits most closely with what has a great deal of value-added for your organization and its competitors. Be prepared to offer an extra payment over the first five years you own these operations that's contingent on business growing more rapidly than in the past. If such suppliers are impressed by your potential to gain from such purchases, such an offer can make all the difference.

What competitor copying-improvement opportunities do such acquisitions make possible?

- New offering designs can be more easily and rapidly implemented that require substantial supplier investments.
- Supplier offerings can be made more compatible with one another so that costs and investments required to provide and to use an offering are substantially reduced.
- Value to stakeholders can also be greatly increased by providing more functionality and other advantages through applied work done by your acquired supplier organizations.
- By having produced such a superior offering, industry demand will surge so that more sales will be made.
- Competitors will see a greater potential to participate in the expanded opportunity if they can provide an offering that's roughly competitive in value with your new offering.
- By being willing to supply components and complementary services, your organization will make such competitive shifts easier to accomplish, less expensive, and more attractive to do.
- Your supplier resources will also cause some larger, as well as much smaller, organizations to consider entering your business, enhancing potential customer interest in your offerings, as well.

From a competitive perspective, such a strategy also offers marketing advantages:

- Customers will be more interested in your organization after learning that your components and services are also powering many competitors' offerings.
- You will be able to establish a more credible identity as an innovator and as a highly capable industry expert.
- Those who want to work with "the best" as customers, suppliers, or employees will seek your organization, rendering future innovations more affordable and attractive to make.
- Many people will remember your improved offering as the first, making it a recognized industry standard to which others will have to compare themselves. In addition, they will remember with awe how its great benefits burst on the scene, changing everything.
- If a competitor decides to add an innovative element, many customers are going to seek your firm's reactions to it ... giving you a chance to avoid losing customers to any future helpful innovations by your competitors.
- If a competitor needs your assistance as a supplier to provide any future innovations, you'll have a longer lead time to consider if you want to match or outdo such innovations.

In addition, this strategy provides profit and cash-flow advantages:

- Competitors' purchases from you as a supplier drive your costs down and help reduce how much investment you need to make relative to your revenues to provide for your own needs.
- By increasing how much operating volume you do, your organization will also generate ideas faster for how to improve redesigned offerings than would otherwise occur.
- With higher volume, you will also be able to afford to replace any equipment more often, providing more opportunities to

enhance what you do in profitable ways that also help expand cash-flow.

What's the key lesson? *An industry-leading organization that sincerely wants to accelerate useful innovation can be helped by making it easier for competitors to copy what the leader does by acquiring and improving dominant industry suppliers, so that competitors will focus more resources on faster and more effective copying of the leader's most successful innovations ... thus setting the bar higher for what the leading organization will need to seek to accomplish for itself in innovation.*

Your Lesson Twenty Assignments

1. How could you and your stakeholders benefit because you make it easier for competitors to innovate and copy by acquiring dominant industry suppliers and supporting competitors with these resources?

2. What would have to change about your innovation practices if competitors become more effective innovators due to your organization making it easier for competitors to copy what you do by making components and services available to them?

3. How could you use making it easier for competitors to succeed in copying by acquiring dominant industry suppliers as advantages in stimulating your future innovations?

4. What could you do now to encourage making valuable innovations available sooner from your organization ... before considering the spur of such enhanced competitors more quickly following your innovations?

5. How can you prepare in advance to make any gains in increasing competitors' copying by your organization acquiring dominant industry suppliers even more productive for your organization, your stakeholders, and the industry?

Part Two

Improve
Customer Effectiveness

... walk worthy of the Lord, fully pleasing Him,
being fruitful in every good work and
increasing in the knowledge of God ...

— Colossians 1:10 (NKJV)

Colossians 1:10 (NKJV) encourages us to do what pleases God, being fruitful in doing good works while increasing in knowledge of God. I read this verse as telling us that we should be living our lives to please Him; improving by gaining more knowledge of God through Bible study, prayer, and doing His will; and engaging in more good works in more fruitful ways. For an organization that is seeking to increase fruitful innovation for advancing God's Kingdom, everyone involved needs to help accomplish more in the ways the verse describes. One way we can do that is by increasing the effectiveness of customers in seeking, applying, and encouraging innovation.

What's the key idea behind encouraging competitors to innovate and copy? More innovation and copying efforts lead to better benefits for all stakeholders. In Part One of *Advanced Business for Innovation*, we look at steps your organization can take that will increase innovation in your company, as well as in the industry. In Part

Two, we expand our investigation to include ways that enhancing what customers do will further increase innovation.

Let me explain more of what I have in mind. Howard Gardner is often quoted for his observation that most adults operate with the equivalent of a five-year-old mind, rather than being able to correctly apply the full education they have received. If people are often operating as little children, then the main focus of innovation has to be in helping them avoid the mistakes that such an unprepared person would otherwise make. However, if we can expand what someone can do to reach the effectiveness of an adult expert, we can focus, instead, on multiplying the benefits from that high level of skill and knowledge. When such changes occur, competitors also have to raise their sights accordingly.

While those who favor traditional business theory might criticize *Advanced Business for Innovation* because it doesn't start with customers and end users as the focus, there's a good reason for not doing so. The very first 2,000 percent solution in *Business Basics* relates to expanding the market by 20 times. The ways for doing so are very customer and end-user focused. The fourth complementary 2,000 percent solution, the one described in *Advanced Business*, pays considerable attention to increasing customer and end-user benefits.

In this part of *Advanced Business for Innovation*, five lessons focus on ways that customers can become effective users of more advanced capabilities and benefits. Lesson Twenty-One emphasizes that helping customers to learn has to be credible and appealing. The search for improving in both dimensions should be never ending. Also, be sure to attract the attention of competitors so that they, too, will seek to educate customers to be better able to use and more eager to apply innovations.

After succeeding with such educational activities, your customers will be better able to appreciate breakthrough improvements that make some attributes of an offering more important, making it possible to shift the competitive landscape in your favor. Lesson Twenty-Two discusses ways that such a changed focus can be accomplished through your company's innovations.

With such better educated and well-informed customers who have shifted their focus to one that favors providing more benefits to all stakeholders, you are ready to take the next step and greatly increase the development information that you share with customers. In the process, your development work will improve from having so much more useful commentary. In addition, what you are doing will be easier for competitors to track and study, thus increasing their innovation and copying activities. These points are covered in Lesson Twenty-Three.

In Lesson Twenty-Four, we explore the importance of leading an industry with authenticity advertising to establish the right kind of an innovation-encouraging relationship with customers so that competitors will be stimulated to do more innovation and copying.

Lesson Twenty-Five advocates directing innovation activities to where value will be exponentially expanded by increasing how many people communicate with one another, an application of Metcalfe's Law. We look at Steve Jobs' relative successes with different offerings to see the potential significance of taking this approach.

Lesson Twenty-One

Educate Customers
In Appealing Ways

For whatever things were written before
were written for our learning,
that we through the patience and
comfort of the Scriptures might have hope.

— Romans 15:4 (NKJV)

Since God first created humans, He has been teaching us to follow the good plans that He has for us. He also tells us through prophets and the Holy Spirit what's coming so that we avoid problems and can be more fruitful. If God is intent on educating us and helping each new generation to learn, we should be that much more focused on supporting His efforts through our organizations providing education to customers.

An innovation-led market will greatly benefit by having educated customers. Otherwise, many customers will stick with the tried and true ... even when it's in their interests to make a change. When such lagged acceptance of improvements occurs, a market develops more slowly and is smaller than it would otherwise be, and fewer benefits are produced for and received by all stakeholders.

Why do some customers resist grabbing hold of the latest advances in innovative markets? In many cases, it's as simple as customers not wanting to take the time to learn what the new benefits and features are.

I'm reminded of a story that Dr. Stephen R. Covey tells in *The 7 Habits of Highly Effective People* (Free Press, Revised Edition, 2004). I condense and paraphrase that story here:

> A visitor encounters a man who is furiously sawing a thick tree by hand. Since the sawing isn't going very well, the visitor suggests that the man sharpen his saw. In exasperation, the busily sawing man complains, "Don't bother me. Can't you see I'm too busy sawing to have time to sharpen my saw?"

As this story indicates, the more someone needs an improvement ... the less likely some of such people will be to take the time to learn about and to make the improvement. After all, they can't get everything done now. They are very busy!

Some customer reluctance to learn about potential changes is based in sound judgment. Companies sometimes tout "big changes" that really don't amount to much. Wait a little while, and customers know that another "big change" will be coming that also isn't very important, except in the minds of the company's marketing staff.

So innovators must become and remain credible with customers.

I believe that another key challenge is making education about the changes interesting and rewarding for customers. In this regard, I'm reminded of the wine market in the United States during the 1970s.

At that time, most domestic wine was fortified by adding more alcohol so that such beverages could have a cost advantage over the more highly taxed grain-based forms of alcohol in providing a cheap high. A few fine wines were also produced using varietal grapes in California, but hardly anyone knew what a Cabernet Sauvignon, a Pinot Noir, a Chardonnay, or a Chenin Blanc (the most common varieties) wine tasted like.

The confusion was increased by the custom of better-known European wine makers using label terms that usually referred to where the grapes were grown rather than to their varieties. As a result, some people who knew what French, German, and Italian wines they liked could not translate that knowledge into picking a similar California wine.

California wine makers slowly overcame this problem by making wine tasting a popular activity. Rather than wait for customers to buy a bottle of wine that they might not like, the California wine makers encouraged potential customers to take a small taste of different wines until they found one that pleased their palates. For many years, this method was so successful in generating sales that such tastings were offered at no charge. Later, the popularity of doing so allowed vintners to charge visitors for tasting higher quality wines.

As more wine makers in California's Napa and Sonoma counties began providing such tastings, the number of people taking a day or a weekend to engage in such tastings greatly increased. Some people even flew in to join the fun. Competition rose among vintners to provide better tours, tastings, and experiences. Everyone benefited.

To encourage copying of its best method for educating customers, an innovator needs to first demonstrate that its educational efforts are highly productive. Competitors are likely to be quick to notice when you enjoy faster rates of growth in revenues, acquiring new customers, and upgrading to the latest offerings by your existing customers. In addition, competitors who lose customers to an innovator with an effective education program will be highly likely to receive recommendations from their salesforces that such an educational program be added or improved.

How can an organization gain an advantage through educational programs? Start by finding what appeals to those who are most interested in learning about any and all improvements in capabilities and benefits. Those people and organizations are the so-called early adopters who play such a large role by steering industries in new directions.

Such customers crave innovation and will try almost anything that can be delivered. Their interest will actually be increased if they can participate while the improvements are being made.

Such people are often important to influencing the rest of the market because many customers will wait to hear that a "lead steer" user has started employing an innovation before considering it. In many cases, such a "wait and see" approach makes sense where a customer often receives smaller benefits from innovations and isn't as skilled at assessing innovations as the customer would like.

If you would like to know more about various customer characteristics in innovation-driven markets, I recommend *Crossing the Chasm* (HarperBusiness, Third Edition, 2014) by Geoffrey A. Moore.

I believe that the preferred means of customer education will vary quite a bit from industry to industry depending on how substantial the advantages are from innovations and the customers' accustomed learning styles. Again, just ask customers to find out.

And encourage current and potential customers to sooner learn more. Changing attitudes in such a way will condition the market to look for more and better innovations from your industry.

Don't hide what you do. Encourage reporters to attend and cover your educational programs, thus providing early access for media reports that your competitors will be likely to study.

Regularly ask current and potential customers to tell you how you can improve your educational activities and how what you do compares to competitors' activities. Such improvements are important because you want to make the market as hungry for innovations as possible, and your competitors' educational efforts will help make that possible.

Keep improving the desirability of what you offer. Invite people to attractive locations and provide interesting noneducational activities, as well. Provide extensive experiences with the innovations. Consider making such experiences rival full-scale simulations, as EDS (originally known as Electronic Data Systems) did with its mock-up of a whole town in the Dallas, Texas INFOMART.

What's the key lesson? *Better educated customers will seek and apply more innovations. By increasing and improving education about innovations, your organization will need to become even better at innovating to hold a leadership position. If your competitors see that innovation-oriented education is helping you to gain advantages, they will seek to compete by making more innovations, copying sooner, and improving their educational programs. Such forms of emulation will help increase your organization's awareness of and interest in innovating.*

Your Lesson Twenty-One Assignments

1. What innovations are poorly understood by current and potential customers?

2. How has understanding of innovations been successfully increased before?

3. Who would like to learn more about innovations?

4. What are the preferred learning styles of those who want to learn more?

5. Why are others not yet interested in learning more about the innovations?

6. What would increase the interest of the uninterested?

7. What effective educational programs concerning innovations are competitors using?

8. How can you use increased understanding of innovations to gain market share?

9. What types of educational innovations are your competitors most likely to feel that they must emulate?

Lesson Twenty-Two

Change Customers' Focus

Behold what manner of love
the Father has bestowed on us,
that we should be called children of God!
Therefore the world does not know us,
because it did not know Him.

— 1 John 3:1 (NKJV)

When the Gospel was first preached, for many people the message seemed to be totally different from what had been taught about what the Old Testament reveals. Such reactions weren't the case because the Gospel messages weren't present in the Old Testament but, rather, because of a more secularly based view of what Scripture meant. To attract new believers, the disciples had to explain these unappreciated truths in new ways, so that their actual meaning could be grasped concerning the willing sacrifice of Jesus Christ to pay the price for all sin and His subsequent resurrection.

Aiding customers to grasp innovations sooner and more fully also requires shifting customers' ways of thinking to more accurately perceive opportunities. When doing so, we should always be gentle, kind, understanding, and patient. Getting the point across is more like offering an encouraging smile than it is nudging someone in the right direction.

Let me explain what I mean by changing customers' focus. If you ask industry customers to tell you about their experiences with all offerings, they will make many different comments and observations. From such responses, you can distill a list of attributes and qualities to which customers most often pay attention. If you then list those most often mentioned attributes and qualities, customers can rank them in terms of their importance in making purchasing decisions and deciding to change suppliers.

Such a ranking of 10 attributes and qualities (with 1 being most important) might look something like this for a machine tool:

1. Low cost of use
2. Simple maintenance
3. Minimal error rate
4. Short programming time
5. Durability
6. Low price
7. Flexibility of use
8. High resale price of used equipment
9. Ease of use
10. Quality of output

Unless there has recently been a technology change in any industry that has been around for some years, it would be unusual for new attributes to show up in the top ten ranked items, and there would be minimal changes in their rank order from year to year. Such stability would reflect offering providers emphasizing gradual improvements to new and existing offerings.

With a strategy of shifting customer focus, your minimum intention would be to move one of the lower-ranked attributes or qualities (say from those ranked 6 through 10) into the top three. Accomplishing this much would be like displaying an encouraging smile to customers. With a strategy of maximum change, the intention would be to shift the whole list so that attributes and qualities not now on the list dominate the ranking. Accomplishing such a result would be the equivalent of taking customers into a new dimension of reality, such as normally occurs during major changes in functionality and effectiveness that involve disruptive change, rather than evolutionary adjustments.

Here's an example of disruptive change. Prior to the invention of the float-glass process for making flat glass, it was very difficult and expensive to make large pieces of glass. The process had changed over the years by increasing the size that could be produced, but not very much in terms of its methods and effectiveness. With the float-glass process (sliding molten silica over molten tin), it was much easier, a great deal faster, and a lot less expensive to make flat glass ... especially in larger sizes. The qualities that a glassmaker cared about after the shift in technology related to the float-glass process, and many of the earlier attributes and qualities no longer mattered. For instance, if you had sold abrasives used to smooth glass in the old process, you stopped making such sales because float glass didn't have to be treated with abrasives to flatten and smooth it.

With a machine tool maker, a possible encouraging-smile refocus might involve making it possible to produce a custom product in a low-cost, automated way for the first time. We saw such a shift recently in book manufacturing. The lithographic printing process requires making at least several hundred books at one time to reduce the fixed costs of production enough to permit a reasonable profit by selling at usual book prices. Printing-machine makers more recently found a way to produce books one at a time on demand at a cost per book similar to making a few hundred with lithographic printing. By reducing how much money was tied up in book inventories, the new process clearly had a major advantage for all titles that weren't going to ever sell several hundred copies ... or at least not that many in a limited amount of time.

While you can attempt to change customers' focus with communications, it's much easier to do so with functional changes that allow your organization to provide different and more desirable results and attributes that have never before been available.

Often this kind of shift can be done effectively by creating offerings that are more specialized. When Amazon.com entered the business of selling its own computers, it did so first by just providing an electronic reading device that allowed storing many books in a more reader-friendly format, Kindle. After someone bought somewhere between 10 and 20 electronic books, the cost of the Kindle reader was more than offset by savings in buying electronic rather than printed books. These electronic reading devices had advantages over smartphones and small computers by being able to display more words at a time than a smartphone while being a smaller handful than most tablet computers. As a result, the Amazon.com electronic reading devices were more conveniently portable than those of their competitors. On trains, airplanes, and buses, such readers soon grabbed a disproportionate share of the market for people who like to read during "dead" time.

If ordinary consumers are your target customers or end users, I believe that most of such refocuses should involve creating custom solutions that better fit into busy, mobile lifestyles. If companies are your target customers or end users, I believe that refocus should be on opening new markets for them to serve greater numbers of customers and end users. Convenience, improved substitutes for existing solutions, and cost breakthroughs are likely to be most important attributes to provide.

A good way to begin is by focusing those who produce new offerings in your organization on the list of customer-preferred attributes and qualities, and then challenging them to develop new offerings that would radically shake up the ranking of the current attributes so that traditional ways of competing would be largely obsolete ... or would soon become so (such as when Amazon.com upgraded a version of its electronic reading device into an inexpensive tablet computer that competes with some functions of the much more expensive and larger iPad). Take what is developed, test it as you do all

138

potential new offerings, and bring out the most promising alternative for the amount of market disruption that you desire in seeking to stimulate competitive innovation and copying. Then pull out all the stops to demonstrate the superiority of your partial or total breakthrough versus the traditional methods.

What's the key lesson? *An industry-leading organization that sincerely wants to accelerate its useful innovations can be helped by developing new offerings that will change customers' focus so much that competitors will feel obliged to innovate and copy.*

Your Lesson Twenty-Two Assignments

1. How could you and your stakeholders benefit because you put in new offerings that will change customers' focus so much that competitors will feel obliged to copy you?

2. If you put in new offerings that will change customers' focus so much that competitors will feel obliged to copy you, what would have to change about your innovation priorities, budgets, processes, and practices to encourage such a circumstance?

3. How could you use putting in new offerings that will change customers' focus so much that competitors will feel obliged to copy you as an advantage in stimulating your future innovations?

4. What else could you do now to encourage making valuable innovations available much sooner from your organization ... beyond putting in new offerings that will change customers' focus so much that competitors will feel obliged to copy you?

5. How can you prepare to make innovation gains from greatly changing customers' focus that increase competitive copying even more productive for your organization, your stakeholders, and the industry?

Lesson Twenty-Three

Share More Development Information With Customers

Then His disciples asked Him, saying,
"What does this parable mean?"

And He said,
"To you it has been given to know
the mysteries of the kingdom of God,
but to the rest it is given *in parables, that*

'Seeing they may not see,
And hearing they may not understand.'"

— Luke 8:9-10 (NKJV)

In Luke 8:9-10 (NKJV), Jesus quotes Isaiah 6:9 (NKJV) to explain that while those who hear His parables will have trouble understanding them, Jesus will explain the parables to His disciples so that they *will* understand. Because the disciples would be carrying the Gospel message to unbelievers after He returned to Heaven, Jesus had good reason to plant seeds in the minds of many with His parables to make it easier for the disciples to later help develop these seeds into the fruit of Salvation.

Similarly, an innovation-encouraging firm should share more of its development plans with customers to gain customers' insights into what is being done, to help prepare customers for what is coming, and to build a stronger bond with customers. While I cannot say if Jesus had any of the same purposes for sharing His parables, I do encourage you to keep His telling of parables in mind as you look into the potential fruitfulness described in this lesson. The practice of introducing new ideas through simple stories is clearly an inviting one that leaves an indelible impression.

The subject of sharing more development information occurred to me after reading reports about the disappointments that many people felt upon learning that Apple had released an upgraded version of its iPhone 4 in October 2011, rather than its much anticipated 4G iPhone 5. Reporters immediately began to speculate how such a common misperception could have occurred.

To me, the answer was simple: Apple preferred to keep customers and end users of its offerings in the dark about what was coming next.

Why would a highly regarded innovator such as Apple adopt so much secrecy concerning its new offerings? Well, there's a long history of technology companies announcing new products that excited customers, consumers, and end users so much that they almost totally stopped buying the current offering. If production or quality problems surfaced with the new model, few would purchase the current product for many months. Without a large cash reserve, a company in such circumstances could go out of business or have to sell itself to a more stable enterprise.

Consider, too, that Apple has often had difficulties in finalizing innovations. The late Steve Jobs was famous for rejecting one "finished" prototype after another. As a result, it could be even longer between announcements and shipments than for many other innovative companies ... causing more danger to a brand franchise and the health of the company's cash flow and balance sheet.

Further, Apple wants to make copying of its innovations as difficult as possible. That decision was expensive in slowing down the development of its Macintosh computer line and in limiting the availability of its superior operating system. Instead, Apple wanted to rely on the demands of Steve Jobs to determine what was innovated, when, and by how much. When Steve Jobs left Apple, the company lost its way. Now that Jobs is permanently gone, it will be interesting to see how the company fares by discouraging, rather than encouraging, copying.

Well, what then should a company do, instead, with its customers to encourage innovation and copying that will stimulate its own organization to be more innovative? Here's a list of six practices to start your thinking:

1. *Ask customers what they like and don't like about existing offerings.* While such questions may or may not identify important needs requiring innovative breakthroughs, having asked the questions will lead customers to become more demanding that improvements be made. More innovation is bound to follow, and sooner, due to having raised customers' expectations.
2. *Involve customers in the development process by letting them know what developments you are working on, what you hope to accomplish, and when you expect to bring an improvement to market.* Doing so will alert your organization when its internal development priorities make no sense to customers. As a result, improved development priorities will probably be established. In addition, the information is very likely to be leaked to your competitors who could be stimulated to accelerate their efforts to match or to exceed your improvements.
3. *Show customers your development work in progress.* Their reactions will help you avoid bringing mistakes to market and missing opportunities to accomplish valuable breakthroughs.

Again, expect the information to leak to competitors, potentially stirring them to greater activity and performance.

4. *Give customers early prototypes to use.* Observe what they do with the prototypes and make improvements based on any opportunities and problems that are identified. You can assume that competitors will also observe or learn about the prototypes in use and draw similar conclusions to yours about what they need to do in order to compete successfully.

5. *Seek large purchase commitments from customers that are tied to meeting development benchmarks.* Such commitments tie up a customer for some period of time. Competitors will feel pressured to match your performance so that they can have at least some sales into each customer account. The effect will probably be to encourage each competitor to narrow its innovation targets to just a few customers for a few innovations. As a result, each competitor will follow along behind you more rapidly ... adding to the incentive for your organization to innovate more often and in more ways.

6. *Regularly report to customers how you are doing in providing what they most want from you in terms of innovations.* Such information flows will make customers more committed to you ... hopefully causing competitors to innovate and copy even more rapidly and effectively.

What's the key lesson? *An industry-leading organization that sincerely wants to accelerate useful innovation can be helped by making it easier for competitors to know what the leader is doing by increasing the development information that is shared with customers, causing more information to leak sooner to competitors, permitting them to focus more resources on faster and more effective innovations and copying of the leader's most successful innovations ... thus setting the bar higher for what the leading organization will need to accomplish in innovation.*

Your Lesson Twenty-Three Assignments

1. How could you and your stakeholders benefit because you make it easier for competitors to innovate and copy by providing more development information to customers?

2. What would have to change about your innovation practices if competitors become more effective innovators and copiers due to your organization providing more development information to customers?

3. How could you use making it easier for competitors to succeed in innovating and copying by providing more development information to customers as an advantage in stimulating your future innovations?

4. What could you do now to encourage making valuable innovations available sooner from your organization ... before considering the spur of such enhanced competitors more quickly following in your tracks?

5. How can you prepare in advance to make any gains in increasing competitors' innovation and copying by providing more development information to customers even more productive for your organization, your stakeholders, and the industry?

Lesson Twenty-Four

Lead with Authenticity Advertising

And a cloud came and overshadowed them;
and a voice came out of the cloud, saying,

"This is My beloved Son. Hear Him!"

Suddenly, when they had looked around,
they saw no one anymore,
but only Jesus with themselves.

— Mark 9:7-8 (NKJV)

Prior to the occurrence related in Mark 9:7-8 (NKJV), Jesus had taken Peter, James, and John to a high mountaintop where He was transfigured. Next, Elijah appeared with Moses, and they spoke with Jesus. Not being sure of what to do or say, Peter offered to build three tabernacles, one each for Jesus, Elijah, and Moses. It was at that moment when a cloud overshadowed them and the voice came out of the cloud commanding them to hear His Son, Jesus. Afterward, Jesus made the three disciples promise not to tell anyone about the events until after He had risen from the dead. His disciples didn't understand then what Jesus was talking about concerning His rising from the dead.

It's hard to imagine a more affirming event than God, the Father, speaking from Heaven to identify Jesus as His beloved Son. While we can't expect to establish our organizations as being bona fide in nearly as authentic and persuasive a way, it's certainly a good idea to do what we can. Authenticity advertising can help.

An early market leader has a major problem: too little advertising to fully stimulate the market's development. In a newer market, profitability may be limited ... even for the market leader ... further crimping the advertising budget. Naturally, those with smaller market shares will often have even less to spend on advertising.

Why is money for advertising so scarce at such times? Well, advertising costs are determined by those who can afford to pay the most for developing effective messages, creating advertising copy, producing ads, and purchasing placements for the ads. Those who are in larger, older markets where most competition is based on advertising executions and spending levels are going to be able to pay much more than those who compete in a newer, smaller, and less-profitable industry.

Advertising has nine helpful effects on an industry that a market leader should seek to encourage:

1. Potential customers become more aware of available offerings and their advantages.
2. Current customers are reminded to purchase.
3. Preferences for a given provider and brand are strengthened.
4. By competitors taking different approaches to attracting customers, a wider variety of potential customers begin to see the industry as relevant to their needs and perspectives.
5. To afford spending more on advertising, competitors will seek to expand their profit contribution margins ... thus reducing price competition that causes unprofitable market-share shifts, which can make innovation less affordable.

6. A new type of offering or feature will move more quickly into wide-scale use, encouraging more consumption and future rounds of innovation.
7. Competitors will seek to differentiate their offerings in ways that will increase the market's size and present your organization with more of a need to stay ahead in innovation.
8. Most industry advertising will be remembered by current and potential customers as coming from the market leader, thus helping to entrench and potentially to expand the leadership position.
9. The company in the industry with the greatest advertising awareness will be able to introduce improved versions of offerings and features after competitors without losing position, as long as the time delay in following isn't too great.

As you have noted, I am also recommending that the market leader employ advertising that emphasizes "authenticity." What do I mean by that? Anyone who has walked around in a major city has been offered low-priced, so-called knock-offs that were designed to look like a highly regarded premium offering, but lacked the materials, workmanship, and authentic brand label to be such an offering. Many people tell funny stories about buying knock-off watches that were branded as a "Rolax" for $50 and having the fakes fall apart shortly thereafter.

As a result of seeing many such scams involving substandard items sold at low prices, those who doubt their ability to tell the differences among offerings will be highly likely to buy from the market leader, drawing comfort from the fact that so many others also buy from that company. An advertising campaign that emphasizes the quality and care of a market leader's activities is highly likely to reinforce the desire of insecure customers to "follow the leader." As an example of this thinking, at one time such concerns about avoiding mistakes helped IBM to gain and to hold an exceptionally high market share of the mainframe computer market.

Naturally, it will be important for such a market leader to act in accord with such advertising claims ... and actually supply superior offerings that are more desirable and reliable.

Such advertising might emphasize the innovations that the market leader provided that are now industry standards. Another point of differentiation can be demonstrating superior ingredients, workmanship, or care. It's especially important to emphasize factors that insecure customers are most concerned about.

Think about such competition over time. Low-market-share and newer competitors need to quickly bring advantages to market. Doing so means that such competitors will more quickly copy the leader and one another. In addition, it means that each such surviving competitor will be highly active in developing new offerings, features, and improvements. As a result, there will be tremendous need for more cash to pay for these activities. To do so, competitors will slash other costs. But they will feel compelled to advertise to keep from being ignored in a market dominated by a leader whose advertising will ultimately quite thoroughly blanket the customers. To afford providing such advertising means competitors becoming even less likely to engage in dropping prices faster than costs decline. Increased advertising expands the market and increases the relative profit and cash-flow gap between the market leader and the trailing competitors. Future innovation succeeds and increases to further encourage the leader and competitors to innovate, making advertising even more effective. And on it goes.

What's the key lesson? *Authenticity-based advertising by an industry leader is highly productive for expanding a market faster, increasing the rate of industry innovation and copying, and supplying more resources to pay for increased advertising and innovation ... creating a virtuous cycle that favors the industry leader and that organization's stakeholders while also richly rewarding all industry stakeholders.*

Your Lesson Twenty-Four Assignments

1. How do current customers in the industry perceive your organization and its competitors?

2. What factors are most important to existing customers in choosing an offering and a supplier?

3. What authenticity concerns do industry customers have?

4. How do potential customers in the industry perceive your organization and its competitors?

5. What factors are most important to potential customers in choosing an offering or a supplier?

6. What authenticity concerns do potential customers have?

7. What advertising claims are being made now?

8. What awareness do decision makers working for customers have about advertising copy and claims?

9. How well is copying of the leader's innovations working for competitors?

10. How well is copying of competitors' innovations working for the market leader?

11. What are the favorite media for current and potential decision makers?

12. How much effect does increased advertising have on expanding the rate of industry growth?

13. What's the optimum level of advertising in the industry?

14. How can that optimum level be reached more quickly?

15. How much of the optimum industry advertising level should be spent by the market leader?

Lesson Twenty-Five

Use Metcalfe's Law

For as the body is one and has many members,
but all the members of that one body,
being many, are one body, so also is Christ.
For by one Spirit
we were all baptized into one body —
whether Jews or Greeks, whether slaves or free —
and have all been made to drink into one Spirit.
For in fact the body is not one member but many.

— 1 Corinthians 12:12-14 (NKJV)

The Apostle Paul tells us in 1 Corinthians 12:12-14 (NKJV) that the body of Christ, the community of all believers in Him, is one. In so saying, part of the message to us is that our individual fruitfulness can be increased by combining our gifts and talents with others in following the directions of the Holy Spirit. The chapter goes on to use the metaphor of a body to show how all of the parts work better together than apart.

A similar lesson can be found in applying Metcalfe's Law to innovation. Let me explain. Before I do, let me again note that this lesson was informed by my reading of *Steve Jobs* by Walter Isaacson.

As I read the book, I was struck by Steve Jobs' strong desire to control everything relating to the user experience. He consistently applied that principle as a way to deliver more value. The approach was probably most successful for iTunes and the iPod. Of the successes Steve Jobs enjoyed, the approach was probably least successful with the original Macintosh computer.

As I thought about Jobs' philosophy of controlling the user experience, I was struck that many other pioneering innovators had adopted the same approach. Thomas Edison and the phonograph immediately came to mind. I once read some of Edison's laboratory notes, and they were a fascinating study in how much control Edison wanted to exercise. He not only determined which music would be recorded, but also the artists and performances. As an opera fan, he would probably be puzzled to learn that "low-brow" music now dominates recordings.

Sometimes, such control is a necessity. When Henry Ford decided to make backward integrations into iron ore mining, steel making, glass manufacturing, power production, and so forth, it was at a time when reliable sources of supply weren't readily available to him in Dearborn, Michigan.

Then I asked the important question of why iTunes and the iPod worked out so much better than the Macintosh computer had. The answer quickly came to me: Metcalfe's Law had a negative effect on the Macintosh computer.

If you don't know what Metcalfe's Law is, let me briefly describe it to you: The observation at its broadest point simply means that the value of ways for communicating exponentially increases with the number of people and devices that can readily communicate with one another.

An example of this law occurred in the market for facsimile machines. The first models were not compatible with one another from one manufacturer to the next. If you didn't have anyone to fax to who had the same machine you had, you couldn't send a fax. I remember this point well, because when we began using facsimile machines between our two offices we had to buy two identical ones ... one for each office. The market didn't really take off until the machine producers agreed on a technical standard that allowed any facsimile machine to communicate with any other facsimile machine.

The Internet has come to be thought of as the ultimate example of Metcalfe's Law, with the increases in the number of users making more kinds of communications attractive and more valuable. Just compare how you communicate now over social media with what you formerly did to contact others you care about.

In the case of iTunes and the iPod, the value of the Apple system doesn't rely on communicating with others. In fact, the only communication involved is the original downloading of music from the iTunes store ... something that Apple made simpler, more desirable, and easier than the alternatives. In fact, many people stopped "stealing" music by sharing what someone else had copied or purchased because the process was more complicated, the music sound quality was worse, and it took a lot more time. As Steve Jobs pointed out, by using filesharing-supplied music you were paying yourself about $4.00 an hour (less than the U.S. minimum wage at the time). In such a closed environment for communications, clearly Jobs' approach was the right one.

Originally, the personal computer industry also involved relatively few communications in those pre-Internet days, and the Macintosh initially gained substantial market share. Most users had the machines at home and used them to play games, to prepare typed documents that were printed out, and to do simple financial applications such as balancing a check book.

With the advent of Ethernet connections, it became possible to link personal computers together in hardwired networks that operated in an office, throughout a building, or even over a business or college campus. If you had a Macintosh, it was easy to communicate with another Macintosh ... but not initially with an IBM personal computer or one of its clones.

Since most business organizations already had IBM mainframes or minicomputers, it was an easy decision to standardize the whole organization on the IBM PC. Some Macintosh machines were still bought by businesses, mostly to be used by those who wanted to do design and desktop publishing work that didn't require real-time machine-to-machine communications.

The first Macintosh had many application programs that also became important to PC users, such as Microsoft Word and Excel. Theoretically, you could use those programs and communicate back and forth quite easily between types of machines. While writing *The 2,000 Percent Solution*, I found that such communications weren't quite that easy with Word. Our coauthor, Robert Metz, had a Macintosh. In 1998, he had to format his file in just the right way or we couldn't use it on a PC after it arrived over the Internet. Even with someone speaking to him on the telephone, this process often entailed 20 to 30 tedious and annoying minutes.

The Macintosh slipped into becoming a machine mostly used by students, writers, and graphic designers. The fewer people who used it, the less incentive there was for software writers to create new applications for it. Priced much higher than PCs and PC clones, few people apparently thought the premium was worth it. Apple was operating in a Metcalfe's Law world with a proprietary product that didn't connect well with the dominant standard, the IBM PC. Metcalfe's Law prevailed.

What do Metcalfe's Law and all this history have to do with you? In deciding what industries to enter, which offerings to provide, and how to structure your business model, seek to add as many communication advantages as possible so that Metcalfe's Law will be an important driver of market growth. For instance, in Lesson Twenty-Eight, I address the importance of establishing an industry standard to encourage copying. If you not only have such a standard, but people also want to be able to communicate with one another, you are in even better shape for encouraging innovation and copying by your competitors: If competitors choose to copy in ways that violate the standard or make communications less effective or more difficult, they will be destroyed. If they innovate or copy as completely as possible in encouraging communications on the industry standard, they will flourish as long as what they provide is priced lower and has some more desirable features.

If you don't yet have an element to your business model that puts Metcalfe's Law to work, you should. You'll find that your competitors will be more reliable copiers and that each copy they provide will increase the value of what you provide to all industry users and customers.

So what's involved in doing so? Here are five key points:

1. Add more reasons for customers and users to communicate.
2. Increase the value of each communication.
3. Make it easier and more pleasant to communicate.
4. Reduce the cost and time of communicating.
5. Educate users and customers about the communications advantages you offer.

What's the key lesson? *An industry-leading organization that sincerely wants to accelerate useful innovation can be helped by making it more important, valuable, and desirable for customers and users to communicate ... encouraging competitors to become better at rapid innovation and copying at lower prices, thus setting the bar higher for what the leading organization will need to seek to accomplish for itself in future innovations that improve and increase communications.*

Your Lesson Twenty-Five Assignments

1. How could you and your stakeholders benefit because you make communications more desirable and valuable for customers and users, providing an incentive for competitors to very rapidly follow your big successes in this regard?

2. What would have to change about your innovation priorities, budgets, processes, and practices if competitors become more effective copiers of your best offerings?

3. How could you use encouraging more and more valuable user and customer communications as an advantage in stimulating your future innovations?

4. What could you do now to encourage making valuable innovations available much sooner from your organization ... beyond what enhancing end user and customer communications can provide?

5. How can you prepare in advance to make any gains in increasing competitors' innovation and copying by enhancing end user and customer communications even more productive for your organization, your stakeholders, and the industry?

Part Three

Encourage Employees

*After these things the Lord appointed
seventy others also,
and sent them two by two before His face
into every city and place
where He Himself was about to go.*

— Luke 10:1 (NKJV)

Luke 10:1 (NKJV) describes how Jesus began sending out pairs of disciples to share the Gospel before He arrived in the places to which they had been sent. In a sense, these disciples were acting much like so-called advance men who precede American presidential candidates during their electioneering. As a result of doing so, Jesus was undoubtedly received by more people and with more enthusiasm, thus allowing Him to accomplish more during each visit.

Unlike *Advanced Business* where all types of stakeholders are explicitly discussed, *Advanced Business for Innovation* specifically considers only customers, end users, and employees. This book is also more limited in that it focuses on just a portion of all innovation tasks. For instance, in this part of the book you won't find much information about things that can be done to directly stimulate innovation and copying among employees who stay with you for the long term. References to strategic decisions in other parts of this

159

book and to rewarding stakeholders described in *Advanced Business* capture some of the many ways to accomplish such stimulation.

Instead, *Advanced Business for Innovation* looks at two of the more powerful ways of encouraging innovation and copying. To appreciate the potential effectiveness of these methods, let me draw contrast with what innovative organizations often do.

Let's imagine that you are a technologist who does developmental work for a company. The firm will probably have you under a contract that limits what you can say and do concerning your work. For instance, in many states your employer will have made it a condition of employment that you would not work for a competitor for some period of time (usually one to three years) after leaving its employ. In addition, you may have been asked to agree not to start a competing firm for the same period of time. Further, the contract may say that you may never use anything you learned at the company for any other purpose.

If all of this agreeing to obey your employer reminds you of serfdom during the Middle Ages in Europe, it should. Many employers try to treat the knowledge and experience of their employees as assets of the firm that cannot be alienated in ways that might potentially harm the company through their being spread.

If, instead, one of your goals is to encourage competitors to innovate and to copy as ways to increase your firm's desire to innovate and effectiveness in this task, naturally, different methods should be taken. Ways of doing so are what we discuss in Part Three.

In Lesson Twenty-Six, you will find the case for releasing employees who seem to be essential to your success to compete when the gain from increased innovation will offset whatever costs and missed opportunities are involved. In this lesson, we also consider ways to be less vulnerable when such individuals leave. The lesson describes some reasons why the actual dangers aren't as great as some people believe.

We then look at how you can stimulate people in your organization, as well as new hires, to develop internal units that innovate and copy what you do for the purpose of expanding the market through adding new users and customers, and lowering prices. In the process, the lure of ultimately becoming leaders of an independently owned entity will usually provide much encouragement. The various steps involved are described in Lesson Twenty-Seven.

Lesson Twenty-Six

Encourage Employees
To Work for Competitors

Then Jonathan said to David,

"Go in peace, since we have both sworn
in the name of the LORD, saying,
'May the LORD be between you and me,
and between your descendants and
my descendants, forever.'"

So he arose and departed, and
Jonathan went into the city.

— 1 Samuel 20:42 (NKJV)

In 1 Samuel 20:42 (NKJV), the Bible relates how Jonathan and David took their leave of one another after King Saul, Jonathan's father, demonstrated that he wanted to kill David. During this parting, it was clear that there would be no room for David to live in Israel while Saul was alive. While this chapter doesn't say where David would go, it's clear that he had no choice but to reside with Israel's enemies. And in later chapters, we see such residency occurring.

While this was a very painful moment for David, it's clear that his leaving Israel was good for God's Kingdom: David, the anointed future king of Israel, would survive, build his skills during this exile, and return to lead the Israelites to great success for which he gave God the credit.

Similarly, having employees leave for competitors can be a positive step for encouraging innovation and copying by competitors, while also stimulating more innovation by your organization. Let me explain.

In most industries, companies go to great lengths to deny access to their employees for any purpose. Employees with higher value-added jobs are often asked to sign employment agreements that don't permit them to work for a competitor after leaving the firm until months or years pass. Lists of employees' names, internal telephone numbers, and e-mail addresses are closely guarded, so that hiring agents such as so-called headhunters will have a difficult time identifying and contacting the most valuable employees. Some organizations go so far as to permit few employees to speak at or to attend external meetings where they might meet competitors.

The logic behind such restrictions is usually two-fold:

1. Concern that the company's secrets and know-how might be disclosed prematurely to a competitor
2. Wanting to avoid the high costs of finding and training someone to replace an effective employee who leaves

As you can see, these two purposes underlying the restrictions are based, in part, on avoiding lost revenues and added expenses. While I don't want to argue that organizations should always encourage employees to leave and work for competitors, I do want organizations to also consider the likely benefits of encouraging more innovation by the organization as an offset to the obvious costs and potentially lost revenues when employees join competitors.

Why do I make this argument? Can you think of any better way to encourage competitors to innovate and copy what your organization does than by their having hired and been influenced by more of your former employees?

Such an idea may not make much sense to some businesspeople. To help with understanding what I have in mind, let me describe four examples of when losing an employee to a competitor might be very beneficial for encouraging a firm's innovations:

Example One: Let's assume that an executive has been developing your firm's new offerings for many years and has done well for you. However, in the last five years the executive has been unwilling to work on a full range of potential offerings, preferring to focus on just one area. Your organization has three excellent internal candidates to replace this executive.

If this executive were to leave for a competitor, he or she would probably carry the same preferences for developing offerings to the competitor. To compete, your organization would have to become more nimble in developing new offerings in this same area. If your organization has three high-potential areas to work on, responsibilities might be distributed among the three excellent internal candidates. The one who is most talented in the former executive's area of focus should receive that assignment. Monitoring should occur to speed quickly improving on any innovations that the competitor brings out. The costs and disruptions following from such a shift would probably be minor after a few months, while the new offering stream for your organization would probably be much greater by the end of two years. Unless the competitor has major brand, distribution, or cost advantages, its improved stream of new offerings in just one area probably wouldn't do much harm to your organization and its stakeholders. In fact, the net effect might be mostly to expand the market and create more interest in your organization's next improvements in this area.

Example Two: A manufacturing executive in your organization has been very innovative in reducing costs through reengineering the organization's production process. This executive intends to become head of manufacturing for a small competitor. There are no strong internal candidates available to replace this executive.

In this case, there's the potential to lose momentum in reengineering and to allow a competitor to gain it. In addition, some operating efficiencies might be lost for a time in manufacturing. So the evaluation of whether the benefits for increased innovation and copying overcome the costs is more difficult.

If everyone in the industry is using equipment developed by your organization, the chances are limited of your organization being quickly overtaken in costs. Also, reengineering produces improvements and cost reductions more slowly than by developing 2,000 percent solutions. If your organization is large enough either to train a 2,000 percent solution tutor or to employ one as a consultant, the same amount of effort aimed at making 2,000 percent solutions in process improvements and cost reductions can potentially produce more valuable results than reengineering did. If you put in place good efficiency metrics for manufacturing, you should be able to maintain effective control by addressing the problem areas so that not as much reengineering will be needed immediately. While there will be some increased costs initially in this case, it's highly likely that the net effects on profitability and cash flow will be positive within a year.

Example Three: A marketing executive who manages your organization's most successful offering intends to start a consulting firm that will work with all of your organization's competitors. There is no strong internal replacement available, but several people could be ready in two years.

This example presents a clear case where near-term costs will be higher because an external person will need to be hired or the job will need to be split among those who can be ready to handle the whole job in two years. Invariably, a new person will want to work on a developing a better marketing program. Doing so will be costly. If, in fact, the new marketing program is a better one, the increased costs will be easily overcome at some point in time. If an independent review of the marketing program shows that there's plenty of room for improvement, changing marketing leaders could be very positive. If all competitors are willing to hire your marketing executive, chances are good that she or he will need to develop marketing programs for each one that will be complementary to one another, rather than identical. If such work is done well, the industry's growth may accelerate due to having a better set of marketing programs that appeal to more types of potential customers in more ways. In such an outcome, there will be less risk of volume and profit loss by your organization.

Example Four: A national-accounts salesperson leaves your organization and immediately begins calling on the same accounts for a competitor. Even the worst salesperson will normally be able to transfer somewhere between 10 and 45 percent of such accounts. However, seldom will the losses exceed 60 percent.

In such an instance, there's clearly going to be a near-term loss of revenues and income. To regain many of those accounts, something about what your organization does is going to have to be greatly improved. What could be a better source of encouragement for innovation? I can well imagine your company's leaders asking about daily progress in recapturing the lost accounts. Assuming that innovation is relied upon rather than price slashing, the effects can be good after a bit ... especially if the innovations lead to increased purchases from the recaptured accounts ... and such innovations can also be used to gain new accounts and to expand purchases from other existing ones.

Let's look at five other potential benefits that aren't covered by these four examples. In doing so, I share my own observations and experiences:

First, most company leaders are closed to changing anything about what they are doing. The more firmly and narrowly such a view has been expressed, the greater the potential benefits after the person goes elsewhere. Almost any individual knows and can accomplish a lot less than what a broader group of people knows and can do. By providing a more inclusive form of leadership, innovation should normally increase quite a bit following such a departure.

Second, many business concepts and practices don't translate very well into a new environment. The competitor's culture may be different, the competitor's issues may lie in another area, or scale effects may limit applicability. A high percentage of external hires for most senior jobs don't work out very well for one or more of such reasons. As a result, the actual harm from a better informed competitor is usually a lot less than was initially feared.

Third, having someone leave often opens the door for someone else to shine whose superior talent wasn't previously appreciated. If such a person felt underestimated by the person who left, there's considerable incentive for the person who remains to perform well.

Fourth, whatever someone knows and understands about your organization quickly becomes obsolete. As a result, incorrect conclusions may be drawn that wouldn't have been made by someone who felt that he or she had more limited knowledge of the organization.

Fifth, someone who is parachuted in to lead a major activity at a competing organization due to supposedly having greater skill and knowledge may well cause a lot more resentment than cooperation among her or his new colleagues. If that's the case, that competitor may well take a step backward as the opposing sides battle it out for supremacy.

Finally, if your organization chooses to be willing to lose any employee to competitors, three practices can help reduce the near-term costs whenever such shifts occur:

1. Have two or more people with higher potential ready to step in.
2. Use discretionary funds to accelerate innovation activities in the biggest opportunity areas whenever a key person leaves for a competitor.
3. Cover major accounts with several sales and support people so that customer relationships will be harder to lose if one of these people leaves to join a competitor.

What's the key lesson? *An industry-leading organization that is willing to lose key employees to competitors can use such personnel changes to encourage and to direct more innovation. By being better prepared for such occurrences, the potential near-term losses can usually be kept quite small and the longer-term gains increased.*

Your Lesson Twenty-Six Assignments

1. How would the loss of each of your most valuable employees to a competitor affect your revenues and costs in the near term?

2. What could you do today to reduce any potential lost revenues and increased costs from such an employee leaving for a competitor?

3. How could you use losing each person to improve valuable innovation?

4. What could you do now to make such valuable innovations available sooner ... without first losing any valuable employees?

5. How can you prepare in advance to make any such employee shifts even more productive for your organization, your stakeholders, and the industry?

Lesson Twenty-Seven

Encourage Employees
To Take Units Public
That Copy Your Offerings

Hold fast the pattern of sound words
which you have heard from me,
in faith and love which are in Christ Jesus.
That good thing which was committed to you,
keep by the Holy Spirit who dwells in us.

— 2 Timothy 1:13-14 (NKJV)

The Apostle Paul instructs in 2 Timothy (NKJV) how to minister to a congregation. In 2 Timothy 1:13-14 (NKJV), Paul tells Timothy to remember what he has been taught and to be strengthened by the Holy Spirit to do what he knows should be done. Similarly, we can expect that those who have worked with us and have been granted unusual opportunities will often adhere to our teachings. When such learning relates to innovation and copying, much more of both can be expected to follow.

From conducting research into what encourages managements to take bold moves that work well, I never fail to be impressed by how much some business leaders will accomplish when given an unexpected opportunity to lead a public company. I believe that this encouragement can be applied to the concept at hand: stimulating competitors' innovation and copying by 20 times to increase your organization's innovation.

Here's what I have in mind.

First, share with your management team that you want to encourage innovation and copying of what your organization does by competitors. Ask for suggestions for how best to do so.

Second, carefully review any suggestions you receive, especially looking for two kinds of responses: those that are high-quality ideas for encouraging existing competitors and those that are high quality ideas for setting up in-house copying competition.

Third, those who submit high-quality ideas for encouraging existing competitors should be asked to keep thinking along those lines. If possible, give these people a role in implementing any of their suggestions that interest you.

Fourth, anyone who suggests setting up internal competition is probably a good candidate for the program that I'm about to describe. Keep any such individuals in mind for this program.

Fifth, if no one suggests setting up internal competition, ask if anyone would be interested in being involved in such an activity. If you have any strong interest, proceed to the next point. Otherwise, look for people who might be interested among any external applicants you have for senior positions.

Sixth, take those who are interested in setting up internal competition and solicit their ideas for how to start. Look for those who want to copy a lot of what you do now and aim some copying at applications in different market segments with lower price points. These people have the right mind-set to accomplish what you want done. If you receive such suggestions, start planning to set up something reasonably similar to what has been suggested by the people you want to do the innovating and copying.

Seventh, establish a budget for the activity that will require heavy reliance on copying what your organization does now.

Eighth, if the unit does a good job of copying and rolling out its first offerings, provide a new incentive: When sales reach $X and profits are $Y, you will set up an autonomous internal unit as a separate corporation with its own board of directors. The potential for gaining internal recognition will be significant.

Ninth, if those objectives are met, next offer to take the separate corporation partially public when sales reach $10X and profits are $10Y. As part of the offer, allow the senior members of the unit to buy stock and acquire stock options at founders' prices. It is at this point that you should expect to see interest in doing more innovating and copying greatly increase ... along with appropriate actions.

Tenth, if those objectives are also met and maintained, then offer to sell more of your company's shares, so that your organization will be a minority shareholder should the unit be able to meet still higher levels of sales and profits.

Finally, if the even higher objectives are also met, offer to sell all of your company's shares so that the unit can become a fully independent public company.

If all has gone smoothly, you should now have added a successful competitor that frequently copies what you do and has a strong desire to show itself to be superior to your organization. Useful innovation and good copying should follow. Your remaining colleagues will also probably feel motivated to show they can be more innovative and successful than the copying organization.

In addition, you may well find that some of your remaining colleagues will someday ask you if they, too, may have an opportunity to repeat what the leaders of the independent copying organization did. Be sure to say, "Yes," while applying any lessons learned from launching the first innovating and copying organization.

What's the key lesson? *An industry-leading organization that sincerely wants to accelerate useful innovation can be helped by making it easier for its own employees to copy what it does in the process of becoming independent competitors ... thus setting the bar higher for what an* *industry-leading organization will need to seek to accomplish for itself in innovation.*

Your Lesson Twenty-Seven Assignments

1. How could you and your stakeholders benefit because you make it easier for your employees to become competitors by improving on and copying what your organization now does?

2. What would have to change about your innovation practices if competitors become more effective innovators due to your turning employees into competitors?

3. How could you use making it easier for competitors to succeed in innovation and copying by turning employees into competitors as an advantage in stimulating your future innovations?

4. What could you do now to encourage making valuable innovations available sooner from your organization ... before considering the spur of creating such enhanced competitors that follow quickly?

5. How can you prepare in advance to make any gains in increasing competitors' innovation and copying by encouraging employees to become effective competitors even more productive for your organization, your stakeholders, and the industry?

Part Four

Stimulate Competitors
To Do More
Innovating and Copying

*Then Saul, still breathing threats and murder
against the disciples of the Lord,
went to the high priest and asked letters
from him to the synagogues of Damascus,
so that if he found any who were
of the Way, whether men or women,
he might bring them bound to Jerusalem.*

*As he journeyed he came near Damascus,
and suddenly a light shone
around him from heaven.*

*Then he fell to the ground, and
heard a voice saying to him,
"Saul, Saul,
why are you persecuting Me?"*

*And he said,
"Who are You, Lord?"*

> *Then the Lord said,*
> *"I am Jesus, whom you are persecuting.*
> *It is hard for you to kick against the goads."*
>
> *So he, trembling and astonished, said,*
> *"Lord, what do You want me to do?"*
>
> *Then the Lord said to him,*
> *"Arise and go into the city, and*
> *you will be told what you must do."*

— Acts 9:1-6 (NKJV)

The beginning of the conversion of Saul of Tarsus, a fervent Pharisee and opponent of Christians, into becoming the most effective missionary of the Gospel to the Gentiles is well captured by this dramatic passage in Acts 9:1-6 (NKJV). After these events, Jesus left Saul blinded to think things over for three days before sending Ananias to share what Jesus wanted Paul to do, restore his sight, help him become filled with the Holy Spirit, and then baptize him.

Even before we consider supernatural powers and effects, these verses remind us that evidence can be so powerful and compelling that no one who has had the experience will mistake or forget its import. I was reminded of this lesson just yesterday while attending a Bible study based on Mark 8:14-9:1 (NKJV). In these verses, Jesus rebukes His disciples, especially Peter, for not seeing clearly and accepting the evidence of the miracles and teachings that He had provided. During the discussion of these verses, many argued that Jesus was prepared for people to take a long time to come to faith. Remembering Acts 9:1-6 (NKJV), it was clear to me that while Jesus is patient because He loves us, He knows that we can come to faith quickly if we are fully honest with ourselves about what we have seen, experienced, and learned.

Learning from the lessons in Part One of *Advanced Business for Innovation* can be thought of as being somewhat similar to learning general lessons that people receive about the Gospel, but as applied, instead, to innovation. As with the Gospel, the message won't sink in for everyone. At the same time, those who get the message will be eager to take the right actions for increasing innovation and copying. When the message sinks in, some will be ready to cooperate in appropriate, legally permissible activities.

Let me again caution you that the legal limits of what you can do with competitors will vary from one country, and from one jurisdiction, to another. So don't assume that because you find a possible action outlined in a lesson here that it will be permissible where you do business. Get good legal advice before doing anything.

That being said, it's my impression that every lesson in this part can be legally applied somewhere. Otherwise, I wouldn't have included the ideas.

What's different here from Part One is that there will be various forms of cooperation taking place between your organization and a specific competitor. Naturally, no competitor will want to do all of these things. Some competitors may not want to do any of them, even if they are legal. So think about these lessons as representing a broad range of possible ways to cooperate, many of which can be combined with one another to accomplish even more.

We begin in Lesson Twenty-Eight by exploring the benefits for an industry, its customers, and an early technical leader that follow from improving an industry's technical standards. Since developing such standards requires much negotiation with competitors, and potentially sharing of intellectual property, no such standard will be established without cooperation from hopefully far-sighted competitors.

We then turn in Lesson Twenty-Nine to developing and licensing standard equipment to competitors. This approach has many advantages, including improvements in customer and end-user experiences. In addition, such equipment can encourage competitors to do more innovation and copying by lowering their costs and reducing the time needed for them to do so.

Providing licenses of your intellectual property to competitors is the subject of Lesson Thirty. We look at the benefits from doing so for everything from market development to adding knowledge that will help your organization to become more innovative.

Lesson Thirty-One builds on Lesson Thirty to emphasize the ways that freely licensing competitors and requiring that certain features be included when using the licenses can accelerate market development and market-share gains. We also consider the moral duty to make any such requirements advance the interests of all industry stakeholders.

Letting others "knock off" your offerings is the notion behind letting competitors "clone" what you provide to customers. While this sounds like a quick way to start a price war and then to lose the competitive battle, the potential benefits for market expansion, increased innovation, and greater copying are enormous. Look carefully at the possibility of using this strategy while retaining enough competitive insulation to prosper, the subject of Lesson Thirty-Two.

In Lesson Thirty-Three, we consider a similar approach: Let competitors sell your company's offerings to their customers. While this may sound suicidal, companies that have done so have often seen market growth increase, profit margins expand, costs decline more rapidly, and innovation develop far beyond expectations. This lesson explains why and how such benefits can accrue.

Another approach to increasing industry innovation and copying is by developing brands that you sell to competitors that have difficulty doing so. Such a strategy is discussed in Lesson Thirty-Four where we look at an example to see how market expansion and innovation opportunities could be improved by this approach.

In Lesson Thirty-Five, we describe the advantages of joint ventures with competitors to establish stronger relationships, and disseminate key knowledge and skills. Such joint ventures can be of a limited nature or established as full companies with one or more other firms.

Lesson Thirty-Six reverses the thinking of Lesson Thirty-Three about providing offerings for competitors to sell to consider selling your competitors' offerings with their brands attached. Doing so increases the ability of customers and end users to appreciate differences, while expanding the likelihood of competitors for whom you sell feeling encouraged to innovate and copy more so that they can narrow the gap in perceptions between your offerings and theirs.

We next look at how providing important services to competitors can eliminate or reduce any deficiencies that make it difficult for them to innovate, improve on, and copy your offerings. By taking on such tasks, you also increase the likelihood of ideas flowing more freely from your organization to the competitors, enhancing their understanding of the opportunities. We explore these ideas in Lesson Thirty-Seven.

In Lesson Thirty-Eight, we extend the idea of offering services for competitors to training their employees in the key skills needed to become better at innovating and copying your work. While this idea may seem silly in the abstract, I encourage you to think about what this lesson says in terms of benefits for stakeholders while increasing innovation by your organization.

If providing services and training can be so effective, just imagine how much more you can accomplish by acquiring competitors, improving them, and then selling them to new owners as a much more effective innovator and copier. This approach to increasing stakeholder benefits is described in Lesson Thirty-Nine.

Lesson Forty demonstrates the potential of making it very clear to competitors that large profits can be earned by simply copying what you, as the innovator, are doing. The examples of Apple with the Graphic User Interface (GUI) and Verbatim with floppy disks are discussed.

Syndicated research is a great tool for creating a more accurate, common perception of industry needs for improvement through innovation. By encouraging such research, you can help competitors avoid mistakes and help draw them closer to working on what will provide the most benefits for industry stakeholders. In the process, innovation and copying will accelerate, putting your organization under pressure to do more. That's our subject for Lesson Forty-One.

In Lesson Forty-Two, we switch to looking at ways that public-research institutes focused on developing technology can stimulate innovation and copying, especially in a smaller industry.

Expanding the supply of capable employees can do a great deal to expand and improve an industry's innovation and copying. Lesson Forty-Three considers how establishing and supporting university research programs can play such a role.

Lesson Forty-Four begins a miniseries of six lessons about using public contests to develop innovative solutions. You should do your best to make it possible and desirable for competitors to become involved in these contests. In this first lesson, our focus is on cost-reducing solutions.

Our focus shifts to a different kind of public contest in Lesson Forty-Five, combining improvements for the first time in ways that add no costs to the less expensive of the two combined improvements. Once again, competitors will be encouraged to participate.

Lesson Forty-Six features improving design at lower cost. As before, competitors should be given attractive opportunities to enter.

Our next lesson examines ways to provide more convenience in ways that reduce waste and lower costs. I describe the many design flaws in water heaters to demonstrate how substantial the opportunities are. Competitors should also be made welcome as entrants in the contest described in Lesson Forty-Seven.

In Lesson Forty-Eight, we look at sponsoring a contest to develop processes that enable offering providers to make custom goods and services at the cost of mass-produced ones. As before, competitors should be attracted to participate.

The sixth and last contest is described in Lesson Forty-Nine: creating offerings that are quickly fruitful in spiritual and profitable in economic terms for customers and end users. With this approach, many excellent improvements can be added to the results of the earlier contests. Competitors should be welcomed with open arms for their contributions.

This part and the book conclude with Lesson Fifty, exploring ways to expand industry demand far beyond current capacity and considering the advantages of doing so for increasing competitor innovations and copying.

Lesson Twenty-Eight

Create an Improved Industry Technical Standard

Diverse weights and *diverse measures,*
They are *both alike,*
an abomination to the LORD.

— Proverbs 20:10 (NKJV)

Much as we are cheated when the proverbial butcher's thumb is secretly pressed on a scale that's weighing our meat purchase, Proverbs 20:10 (NKJV) strongly advises us in contrast to always use accurate measures when dealing with others. While the intent is obviously to encourage honesty, the verse is also dealing with something quite practical, the benefit for everyone of getting exactly what they seek and expect. When an industry adopts a technical standard to help ensure that's the case, both kinds of benefits are generated.

Since technical standards provide many potential advantages for those who succeed in establishing them, I thought that this topic would help provide an easy-to-understand strategy for increasing innovation and copying. In most new and emerging industries, there is no existing technical standard. The firms that initially serve customers usually propose and follow their own proprietary standards, hoping to convert the rest of the market after customers show a preference for their solutions.

While such an approach seems optimal to managers who believe they will eventually prevail, competing standards often don't do anyone much good. Customers purchase less than they might due to being concerned about potential obsolescence. Competitors following standards that lose out are on a fast slide into oblivion, wasting knowledge, resources, and talent in the process. Typically, the "winning" standard among several proprietary ones will often have many weaknesses that delay market development. The early experience with supplying offerings may not transfer into applying the ultimate standard, meaning that costs may be higher and features less attractive than they might otherwise be.

Competition in any large market over the long run isn't going to have anything to do with the technical standard unless one organization has a headlock on virtually all of the relevant patents. Otherwise, markets mostly respond to competitive differences in factors such as distribution, availability, quality, awareness, image, features, ease of use, pricing, service, and economic benefits.

A market leader can be greatly assisted by taking the experience of the market's early development to see which aspects of technical standards are proving to be most appealing to the industry's customers. By sharing what has been learned, a company can make a more compelling case to its competitors for what the technical standard should be. Usually, this standard won't be identical to an existing standard but will, rather, combine elements from existing standards as well as some new elements.

While those benefits probably seem relatively clear, there are seven advantages and opportunities that may not stand out as much to you:

1. Once having coalesced into a single technical standard, effectiveness in other factors will become more important to competitive success. In most of such competitive factors, the early market leader will have advantages that will be reinforced by future innovation and copying by competitors.

2. Competitive risk from technological innovations will be reduced. Everyone in the industry will probably have agreed to cross-license one another on key intellectual property rights, such as patents, so that any innovation will soon flow into the offerings of all competitors.

3. If the resulting technical standard was mostly reached due to your organization's leadership, many customers will first seek your advice in the future about what the technical migration path will be. As a result, you will be the first to know about new influences that have the potential to shift the competitive balance.

4. Once a technical standard has been set, potential partners will mostly focus on teaming with you ... rather than with a competitor. That's because your relative advantages in serving the market will be increasing and this position will be highly visible to potential partners.

5. Competitors that must make more substantial shifts to apply the new technical standard will experience a period of time when revenues decline and many operational adjustments will have to be made. Many of such organizations won't be able to handle the shift very well, and they may also end up with substantial ongoing costs to support existing customers through their proprietary standard.

6. When you make shifts in the future that enhance some aspect of applying the industry's technical standard, competitors will be highly eager to at least match what you do ... if not find a lower-cost way to achieve a similar result. You can then study their solutions to identify how to improve your innovation in ways that you might not have considered. As a result, the more copyists you have, the more you can potentially learn. With a greater scale of operations, you will usually be better able to apply this knowledge than competitors.

7. If the standard is established early in an industry's life, more competitors will survive than if it takes longer to develop such

a standard. That's because customers will be more willing to buy from a wider number of suppliers. The effect is to raise the average cost of producing an offering in the industry. When that occurs, the potential for a higher profit margin is increased. Seeing that potential will draw more financial support for competitors so that they will have greater funds to look for innovations that you can seek to exceed by combining practices that individual firms haven't put together before (thus, exceeding the future best practice).

What's the key lesson? *By focusing industry development on one technical standard, an early industry leader will shift competition toward factors from which the leader will benefit.*

Your Lesson Twenty-Eight Assignments

1. What features about other companies' technical standards do customers prefer to your company's standards?

2. What features about your company's technical standards do customers prefer to other companies' standards?

3. What is missing from existing technical standards to bring many more purchasers into the industry?

4. What aspects of technical standards should be added to increase the amount of copying of your approaches and innovations that competitors will do?

5. What competitive strengths will be most important for your organization to increase before, during, and after an industry technical standard is set?

Lesson Twenty-Nine

Develop and License Standard Equipment To Competitors

"You have heard that it was said,
'You shall love your neighbor
and hate your enemy.'
But I say to you, love your enemies,
bless those who curse you,
do good to those who hate you,
and pray for those who
spitefully use you and persecute you,
that you may be sons
of your Father in heaven;
for He makes His sun rise
on the evil and on the good,
and sends rain on the just
and on the unjust."

— Matthew 5:43-45 (NKJV)

In these verses, we can begin having a new understanding of God's perspective, one that we are to adopt: Love one and all unconditionally, just as He does. While some believers find it hard to love, pray for, and do good to their enemies, many businesspeople find it even harder to think about being similarly loving and kind to competitors. Yet, there are Earthly blessings for doing so. In the Bible, Jesus is silent on the subject, but it may be that He views your competitors as somewhat analogous to the enemies He spoke about as reported in Matthew 5:43-45 (NKJV).

Whether you manufacture a product or provide a service, it's likely that some improved equipment can enhance your offerings by enabling you to produce greater quantities or provide even higher value. Most industries expand much more slowly than their potential due to the lack of highly effective equipment. In the absence of such productivity-enhancing or value-improving capabilities, many activities are done less well and in higher-cost ways than are desirable. In addition, there may be offering delays that discourage customers from buying. Further, if customers are very disappointed in what they receive, any potential willingness to purchase may be permanently erased. Or word of mouth comments about unsuccessful experiences with an offering can create a road block to even considering trial by those with no current interest.

Let me provide two examples to help you better understand what I'm addressing, starting with Kentucky Fried Chicken (KFC). As originally conceived, the product's uniqueness came from two characteristics: a tangy combination of spices in the flour coating the chicken that added flavor and faster production by using pressure cookers. As anyone who has used a pressure cooker knows, it's hard to reach just the right result. Bigger pieces of chicken take longer to cook while smaller pieces require less time. In the same pressure cooker, there's a potential to under- or overcook every piece. You also can't see the chicken to determine whether it's done or not. As a result, many customers actually received undercooked and overcooked pieces of fried chicken that displeased them.

KFC's chiefs knew they needed a more consistent result and began commissioning equipment companies to produce fryers that would correctly cook each piece of fried chicken. Such equipment brought new problems. So much chicken was produced in a batch that it could not be sold quickly enough to remain fresh. Customers were usually getting chicken that wasn't as fresh as before, dried out and unappealing looking after being under heat lamps for too long. In addition, the equipment wasn't easy to clean. Cleanliness declined with inevitable impacts on product quality.

Competitive vulnerability increased as other fast food chicken operators simply made conventional fried chicken in deep fryers. By producing smaller batches, their chicken was fresher and hotter. Cooks could simply rely on their eyes ... aided by timers ... to decide when the chicken was ready.

Let's next consider a service, cataract surgery. Physicians have long known what a cataract is, but they struggled for many centuries to locate ways to remove cataracts that would restore pre-cataract vision. The latest breakthrough came when implantable intraocular lenses were developed. To make the most of this innovation, measurement equipment had to be developed so that the right type of lenses would be implanted. In addition, equipment had to be developed to produce such lenses in high quality, low cost ways.

If every eye surgeon had used different equipment, costs would have been much higher and quality would have been lower. In addition, patient outcomes would probably have been much worse.

As you can see from these two examples, industries continually go through transitions from one way to supply customers' needs to methods that are intended to provide more customer benefits. In the process of making such shifts in methods, it's not unusual for improved equipment to be needed. Although it may be of immense value for an industry to have such superior equipment, few organizations typically understand what's needed, know how to provide for those needs, and can afford and are willing to spend enough to make the required investments.

When such equipment development doesn't occur or doesn't succeed, major opportunities are missed.

What can be done instead? If your organization is knowledgeable and sufficiently well financed, begin a continuing program of developing any equipment that might deliver better customer or other stakeholder benefits, reduce costs for all stakeholders, or eliminate stakeholder investments. Don't expect that you will produce the ultimate equipment in one design generation. More typically you should expect to go through dozens of design generations before reaching anywhere near the full potential. That's because each generation of designs presents new opportunities to learn from experience, to simplify, and to add more performance dimensions.

Here's an example. A number of years ago laser printers for personal computers first became affordable. A good printer cost about $4,000 and provided beautiful pages. What a delight! Ink-jet printers hung around by being much less expensive than laser printers and delivering quality that wasn't too obviously lower.

When one of our company's $4,000 laser printers stopped working, my instinct was to repair it. A colleague suggested instead that we look into what a new ink-jet printer would cost. That was a good call. Now, we operate with ink-jet printers that are much more compact, require less expensive supplies, produce much better looking print on the pages than the old laser printer ever did, and only cost $99 to purchase. Wow! That shift in performance and price beautifully shows what many generations of equipment-design improvements can do.

Such benefits from repeated design generations can be so substantial that by simply controlling the technology's development, it's possible to establish an outstanding business. Consider Qualcomm, the organization that created CDMA (Code Division Multiple Access) technology for cell phones and provides some of the components (such as chip sets) for mobile telephone companies to operate their businesses. As of this writing, Qualcomm boasts a market value for its stock in excess of $100 billion.

A Qualcomm-type strategy can be very rewarding for encouraging innovation, particularly if there are competing technologies (as there are for Qualcomm in the world-leading GSM, Global System for Mobile communications, standard that was developed by and is favored by Europeans). If customers don't gain enough advantages fast enough, such a competing technology dies out. Through more successful innovation during each design generation, the size of the market and the technology's market share expand. It's a great way to help an organization become more innovative, especially as customers continually make compelling requests for improvements.

If you cannot afford to take as aggressive an approach as Qualcomm has, consider teaming with competitors to pool knowledge, skill, and financial resources to accelerate appropriate equipment developments. Under such circumstances, industry growth can be accelerated in a healthy way while you can shift competitive differentiation into areas that favor an innovative market leader. Since you won't want your competitors to use improved equipment developed by someone else, you can expect to stimulate your organization to be more innovative in cooperating with competitors.

If you temporarily stumble while pooling resources, you can benefit by having cross-licensing agreements with your competitors so that you can access any breakthroughs they make. Having seen that you have fallen behind and are making royalty payments to competitors will also nudge your organization into become more competitive with its innovation activities.

Naturally, you will probably want to retain a few proprietary methods that are not immediately available to competitors. Be sure to have a timetable for ultimately releasing any such advantaged methods to competitors as an encouragement for developing still more effective proprietary advantages embodied in new, specialized equipment.

What's the key lesson? *Developing and licensing superior standard equipment by an industry leader to its competitors can be highly productive for expanding a market faster and increasing the rate of its own innovations.*

Your Lesson Twenty-Nine Assignments

1. What equipment features would help your company to expand much more rapidly through accelerating market growth, reducing stakeholder costs, and eliminating stakeholder investments?

2. Is your organization capable of developing such equipment advantages on its own?

3. Who else can help you accelerate innovation involving helpful features?

4. Can your organization afford to develop such equipment on its own?

5. If you develop your own equipment, will competitors be willing to purchase or license your equipment?

6. If your organization cannot afford to make such developments or competitors would be unwilling to buy from you, are competitors willing to join with you in this activity?

7. Can you obtain cross-licenses from competitors for any future improvements they make?

8. How else can your relationships with competitors be structured to accelerate your organization's equipment innovations?

Lesson Thirty

License Your Intellectual Property To Competitors

Do not be deceived, God is not mocked;
for whatever a man sows,
that he will also reap.

— Galatians 6:7 (NKJV)

The secular theory for legally protecting intellectual property is based on the assumption that the economic gains from having exclusive rights are essential to encouraging development of such advances. In practice, that assumption is not always the moving force. Just last night, I discussed with someone how eagerly many poets develop their craft, despite knowing that there will be little or no economic compensation from their copyrights. For many poets, the experience of creation is a satisfactory reward. Some creative people in all fields are similarly motivated.

Galatians 6:7 (NKJV) and the following verses remind us that there are eternal consequences for us and others from what we produce and share. Produce in accord with the Holy Spirit, and spiritual gains will be yours. So in addition to considering the gains that we receive, we should also estimate the potential impact on God's

Kingdom and on the benefits that He wants to be more readily received by all of His children.

While we may have the legal right to not share intellectual property that our organizations have developed, God surely wants the results of the minds He has given to and developed in us to be used to help others in as many ways as possible.

As we discuss concerning establishing industry standards in Lesson Twenty-Eight, a great way to improve market development is by creating a common base of technology. This approach is especially important in industries where innovation is going to be a significant activity. No one wants to take a chance on building a business based on the output of a single supplier. If several others can supply what you do, demand will greatly grow.

In many cases, there either are no competitors to work with in establishing an industry standard or little interest among credible firms in entering a nascent industry. In such instances, the innovating firm will have to lead in establishing intellectual property in the form of patents, trade secrets, copyrights, and trademarks.

With an effective array of such intellectual property producing a profitable result, few may dare to enter until a key patent expires. As a result, innovation may stagnate.

Let's look at an example. I well remember the days when Xerox "owned" the worldwide market for plain paper copiers. The firm wouldn't sell its copying equipment to customers. You had to rent it by paying a price per copy. You weren't even guaranteed to receive a new machine.

With its comfortable monopoly, Xerox did little to reduce its costs. As productivity rose in its Rochester, New York, plants, Xerox sent production workers home earlier and earlier while paying for full-time work. Before long, the work "day" was down to just a few hours. Despite complex designs that jammed the paper quite often, Xerox did little to simplify its machines and improve service.

When the patents expired, Xerox found itself competing with organizations that were selling copiers for much less than it cost Xerox to make theirs. The market boomed as prices dropped and quality improved. Xerox would have greatly benefited by causing that entry to occur sooner, helping to focus it on improvements rather than milking maximum profits at high prices from minimal work.

One of the beauties of encouraging innovation and copying by licensing your intellectual property to competitors is that you can control the timing of when their activities occur. For instance, you can license applying a patent to a specific market or application, rather than making it generally available. This approach can be most helpful when a market is emerging and you don't expect to be able to develop specific offerings for many niches. The competitors' innovations in such circumstances may often provide superior solutions that will have substantial applications in other parts of the market, especially in relationship to cost reductions and value improvements. Since it is standard practice to agree to cross-license such intellectual property, your organization will then have access to any new intellectual property rather than being threatened by it and unable to respond directly.

Depending on how much innovative pressure you want to put on your organization, you can choose, then, to improve on the competitors' innovations from within your own intellectual property or use cross-licenses of intellectual property that competitors develop that's related to your intellectual property.

Xerox did a little of such licensing by providing intellectual property to Rank Organization in the UK and to Fuji in Japan. These rights were limited to geographies outside of North America that Xerox felt initially ill-equipped to develop on its own. The company was later almost literally saved by being able to learn from its Japanese licensee how to design and manufacture equipment less expensively that was also more reliable and less costly to service.

While I could provide many examples of how companies have been helped or hurt by making it easier for competitors to innovate and copy by licensing, I suspect it will be much more valuable for you to know what factors should be considered in deciding what intellectual property to license, for what purposes, and when. Some of these perspectives follow:

Market Development: If your market needs competitors to grow, you would be wise to encourage such market entries. If a particular segment of a market is stagnating or not developing as rapidly as possible, licensing can be a good way to encourage expansion.

Brand Development: If you expect to have global competitors at some point, licensing brands can be very helpful for establishing awareness and image advantages in advance of stronger competition.

Value Enhancement: If your organization is having trouble increasing the usefulness or benefits gained from using your offerings, making licenses available may increase such innovation in ways that will expand the market and grow interest in all of such offerings. If you doubt that you will be able to "invent around" any intellectual property that licensees develop, by all means obtain cross-licensing agreements from your licensees.

Cost Reduction: In many cases competitors have skills in design, process improvement, manufacturing, or services that will enable them to reduce costs for all stakeholders much more rapidly than you can. These are the competitors who are most likely to take away your industry leadership. If you are concerned about that potential risk, I suggest that you propose engaging in joint ventures with them so that you can learn from such a competitor while cost-reducing innovations are created.

Investment Elimination: A competitor might have access to resources that help avoid many costs. In such an instance, providing a license might be an effective bargaining chip for your organization to gain an advantage in this regard.

Company Value Enhancement: In some instances, you may need credibility with the investment community for the value of your intellectual property. When a larger, better-known organization is willing to license your intellectual property, you may well see quite a large increase in what investors will pay to invest.

What's the key lesson? *An industry-leading organization that sincerely wants to accelerate useful innovation can be helped by licensing intellectual property to competitors, so that competitors will focus more resources on faster and more effective innovating and copying of the leader's most successful innovations in areas where the leader is likely to make the least progress on its own ... thus setting the bar higher for what the leading organization will need to accomplish in innovation.*

Your Lesson Thirty Assignments

1. How could you and your stakeholders benefit because you license intellectual property to competitors?

2. What would have to change about your innovation practices if competitors become more effective innovators and copiers due to your organization licensing intellectual property to them?

3. How could you use licensing intellectual property to competitors as an advantage in stimulating your future innovations?

4. What could you do now to encourage making valuable innovations available sooner ... before considering the spur of such enhanced competitors more quickly following in your tracks?

5. How can you prepare in advance to make any gains from licensing intellectual property to competitors even more useful for your organization, your stakeholders, and the industry?

Lesson Thirty-One

Require Licensees to Use Certain Features

He has shown you,
O man, what is good;
And what does the Lord require of you
But to do justly,
To love mercy,
And to walk humbly with your God?

— Micah 6:8 (NKJV)

"Require" is one of those words that can cause many people to bristle. Since most people who require us to do something are looking out for themselves more than for us, such reactions are certainly appropriate. However, Micah 6:8 (NKJV) presents a different kind of requiring, requiring from God Who wants what is best for each person: leading us to focus on the good, acting justly, loving mercy, and walking humbly with Him. While each of us can hardly hope to be as other-centered in requiring certain things be done, we should certainly be doing our best to act in such a way. How to do so is the focus for this lesson.

Once again, *Steve Jobs*, by Walter Isaacson, provides some of the background for this lesson. In 2011, attention was focused on law suits that Apple brought against companies that had copied what it had patented for use in the iPhone. Apple's purpose in suing was to gain market share for its iPhone. As I read about this litigation, I began to ponder how Apple might have gained more by encouraging competitors to copy its patents through licensing them.

The licensing thought occurred to me as I considered that in North America the competing Android operating system for cellular telephones had already gained about 70 percent market share, leaving Apple with about 30 percent. Apple's rapid drop in market share, despite its innovations, made me appreciate, once again, that Apple could end up with a small part of a large market, as occurred with desktop computing.

While licensing others to produce cellular telephones using Apple's technology would certainly cut into potential profits from selling iPhones, Apple has another potential source of revenue that could be much richer: developing its own applications and selling its own and others' applications to cell-phone users.

To succeed, it would be highly desirable that all cellular telephones be able to use the applications that Apple produces and sells. In that way, Apple could have profits from selling applications to the whole market, rather than just its hardware portion of it.

Since patent litigation is quite expensive, much of the expense that Apple incurred could have been avoided ... making further investments in innovation more affordable and attractive to engage in.

To create the most success, such a strategy would require always having the most cutting-edge devices and supporting technology patents and licensees for producing devices that would run the applications that Apple develops and wants to sell. Licenses could be provided on a basis of requiring that certain features be present in all licensed cell phones so that full application compatibility would be in place. The result would be to engage in a strategy much more like what Qualcomm uses in licensing cellular telephone technology for CDMA and selling chip sets and software for using the licenses.

In Apple's case, such an approach could have worked quite easily. Most of the competing "smart" cell phones were built with components that Apple also purchased from the same suppliers. With a slight shift, those components could have been replaced by superior proprietary components that Apple could have controlled and sold to licensees.

The challenge for Apple would have been to decide whether it would have been willing to open up its technology to let a wider variety of application software packages run on it. That approach was always rejected by Steve Jobs in the interests of providing a smoother and more predictable customer and user experience. Clearly, there's plenty of room in the middle between letting in almost any application and letting in fairly few. Now that Jobs is no longer with us, it may well be that new management will at some point be more open in this regard.

Let's look more generically at such a strategy for encouraging copying. First, it can be applied to services as well as to products. A variety of intellectual-property rights (patents, copyrights, trademarks, and trade secrets) can be used to obtain and to maintain exclusivity for a period of time.

Second, it is ideal if such licensing can more rapidly expand a market. That's especially likely to be the case where services are involved because they are typically much more difficult to expand rapidly. When your organization lacks initial credibility with the majority of potential customers and users, adding licensees with high credibility can help, as well, in product markets.

Third, it's even more desirable if you can gain some resource advantages through the larger expansion beyond simply adding licensing revenues. Such advantages can occur by selling components or related offerings (either products or services).

Fourth, it's best if the resulting business model will focus your innovation into a narrower concentration on the most valuable activities for expanding stakeholder benefits. In this way, your expertise will grow more rapidly and its value will also expand faster.

Fifth, you should create an exciting definition of what kind of innovation to do so that all stakeholders will feel motivated to assist you in making faster progress. An example might be engaging in something that will create benefits through emphasizing Metcalfe's Law that energize stakeholders.

What's the key lesson? *An industry-leading organization that sincerely wants to accelerate its useful innovations can be helped by freely licensing its intellectual property in agreements that require using certain features that will expand the market and create opportunities for all stakeholders to benefit from that expansion.*

Your Lesson Thirty-One Assignments

1. How could you and your stakeholders benefit because your competitors can quickly and easily copy your innovations due to freely licensing intellectual property in agreements that require using certain features that will expand the market and create opportunities for all stakeholders to benefit from that expansion?

2. What would have to change about your innovation priorities, budgets, processes, and practices if competitors become more effective copiers of your offerings after you freely license intellectual property in such agreements?

3. How could you use freely licensing intellectual property in agreements that require using certain features that will expand the market and create opportunities for all stakeholders to benefit from that expansion as an advantage in stimulating your future innovations?

4. What else could you do now to encourage making valuable innovations available much sooner from your organization ... beyond freely licensing intellectual property in agreements that require using certain features that will expand the market and

create more opportunities for all stakeholders to benefit from that expansion?

5. How can you prepare in advance to make any gains from freely licensing intellectual property in agreements that require using certain features even more productive for your organization, your stakeholders, and the industry?

Lesson Thirty-Two

Clone Your New Offerings

*Jesus Christ is the same
yesterday, today, and forever.*

— Hebrews 13:8 (NKJV)

The Bible tells us in a variety of ways to become more like Jesus. That's good advice because He is perfect. I often reflect on what He might do when I run into a difficult situation. Doing so is a mental discipline that helps me realize by how far short I fall of His great example. However, by keeping Him in mind, I can come closer to what I should do. I often think how nice it would be if I could become just like Him.

Whenever my thoughts turn in that direction, I'm reminded of how much we like to copy what we think is better. If a slight style shift occurs in frames for glasses, you will soon be surrounded by similar pairs. If someone comes out with a better electronic gadget, many people can't wait to get one. If the "real thing" is expensive, many people shop for a closely resembling item that is less expensive.

Such instincts can be helpful for encouraging innovation within and without your company, as well as for copying from without. Cloning is one way to capitalize on such opportunities.

What do I mean by a "clone" of your organization's new offering? Here are definitions of "clone" as a noun from dictionary.com:

1. Biology
   A. a cell, cell product, or organism that is genetically identical to the unit or individual from which it was derived.
   B. a population of identical units, cells, or individuals that derive from the same ancestral line.
2. A person or thing that duplicates, imitates, or closely resembles another in appearance, function, performance, or style: *All the fashion models seemed to be clones of one another.*

As you can easily imagine, I'm referring to the second definition in terms of a "thing." I'm also stretching that definition a bit to include a service as being a thing.

Let's start by looking at a product example. Do you ever use a PC (personal computer)? If you do, chances are that the equipment you use is a so-called clone of an IBM personal computer.

But chances are even better that you have never used a clone of an Apple Mac computer.

What's the difference? IBM chose to use Microsoft to develop its operating system for the original PC and granted the software maker the right to sell similar versions for non-IBM equipment. In addition, IBM used standard components that anyone else could purchase. Rival microcomputer makers quickly saw that they would sell more machines if they could operate software applications created for the IBM PC ... and so they did. Competitors quickly began to produce PC clones that had superior features (such as more portability), as well as lower prices. The market zoomed. Unfortunately, IBM wasn't prepared for what it had ignited and within not too many years IBM wasn't profiting from its PCs, and sold the business to Lenovo in 2005.

Apple, by contrast, developed its own operating system and for many years would not license producing or using it to anyone other than a Mac user. The company trailed all but the smallest PC clone makers until recently when its base of software applications began to make Macs more effective rivals for PCs.

If a company were to engage in such a deliberate clone strategy today, the same results could be accomplished by providing a full set of technical specifications and directions for providing an offering (whether a product, a service, or a combination of the two), licenses to use the appropriate intellectual property, and any equipment or software essential to gaining the full benefits from making or using a clone.

Obviously, to be successful such clone competitors would have to either introduce value-added innovations or sell for a much lower price. If cost reductions were unlikely (such as in the case of the PC where components were purchased off the shelf from the same suppliers), it's clear that innovation would be stimulated.

In such a circumstance, companies usually cross-license one another. As a result, any innovations that add intellectual property for competitors would become immediately available to your firm, as well. Consequently, industry-wide innovations are likely to more quickly expand the market size.

How does such cloning work in services? As Carol Coles and I describe in *The Ultimate Competitive Advantage* (Berrett-Koehler, 2003), a dry-cleaning supplies distributor used developing service innovations for its dry-cleaner customers as a point of competitive advantage. One such innovation enabled 24-hour-a-day drop offs, making life more convenient for a dry cleaner's customers. The effect of the distributor's innovations was to make dry cleaners both more effective and more similar to one another in their services, except for whatever branding and locations did to differentiate them from one another.

With such a strategy for encouraging innovation, it's important to determine if your organization needs a cushion in time to enable it to stay far enough ahead of competitors. If you do need more of a time cushion, you can always set the initial licensing agreements to provide some flexibility in how rapidly the new intellectual property has to be shared with your competitors. If you failed to reach such an agreement, another approach is to emphasize innovations that require longer preparations before clones can be provided.

Unlike the case where you produce for competitors on a private-label basis, you won't gain nearly as many cost advantages from this strategy of encouraging product or service clones. As a result, this approach provides a more powerful incentive to become more innovative ... just because a loss of position can occur more quickly and to a greater degree.

Knowing that the door is open to the know-how necessary to create and to succeed with clones will be a powerful motivator for competitors to copy innovations that succeed in the market. You'll have your hands full staying ahead of rampant duplication.

What's the key lesson? *An industry-leading organization that sincerely wants to accelerate useful innovation can be helped by making it easy for competitors to clone its offerings, so they will focus more resources on faster and more effective copying of and improving on its most successful innovations ... thus setting the bar higher for what the organization will need to seek to accomplish for itself in innovation.*

Your Lesson Thirty-Two Assignments

1. How could you and your stakeholders benefit because you make it easy for competitors to clone your new offerings?

2. What would have to change about your innovation practices if competitors become more effective innovators due to your organization making it easy to clone your new offerings?

3. How could you use making it easy for competitors to clone your new offerings to improve your own valuable innovations?

4. What could you do now to encourage making valuable innovations available sooner ... before considering the spur of such enhanced competitors more quickly following your innovations?

5. How can you prepare in advance to make any gains from making it easy for competitors to clone your new offerings even more productive for your organization, your stakeholders, and the industry?

Lesson Thirty-Three

Provide Offerings for Competitors to Sell To Their Customers

"Give to everyone who asks of you.
And from him who takes away your goods
do not ask them *back."*

— Luke 6:30 (NKJV)

Jesus is saying in Luke 6:30 (NKJV) that we should give what we have to whomever asks. And if someone takes something without asking, just let the matter go. Let's look at an example. If you have ever read the book or seen the musical *Les Misérables*, you may remember that just after Jean Valjean is released from prison for having stolen a loaf of bread, he is taken in by a Christian bishop. During the night, Jean Valjean steals the bishop's silver and takes off. When Jean Valjean is arrested the next day, the bishop doesn't accuse him of stealing but calls the silver a gift and adds two silver candlesticks to what Jean Valjean had stolen. That fictional event comes pretty close to describing what Jesus was talking about in this verse.

If you have great offerings, your competitors could gain advantages if you produced versions of those offerings that they could sell as their own. What would Jesus do?

You may not be inclined to follow His fine example when it comes to business, but I want to point out some secular advantages that you may not be considering.

If imitation is the sincerest form of flattery, then a competitor hiring your organization to provide your offerings to its customers must indicate a strong preference for your ways of doing business. With such a close relationship, there will naturally be many occasions in which employees from both organizations will need to work together, beginning with determining the designs and specifications for the new offerings. On a day-to-day basis, both organizations will need to be in contact to coordinate activities and to ensure that customers' needs are met. There will be, of necessity, few secrets between the two organizations with regard to these offerings.

As you can imagine, such a close connection will lead to sharing much information and many perspectives. By drawing on your organization's greater resources to innovate through new offerings, competitors will be able to upgrade and to improve much more often. With many fewer activities to do for themselves, competitors will also have more time and financial resources to work on innovations that will push your organization to innovate more effectively and often.

You may be wondering how in the world your organization could possibly provide your competitors' offerings to its customers. That's simple. With products, the answer lies in something called "private label."

Have you ever gone into a supermarket and found that many of the offerings on its shelves carried the store's logo and brand names? While you probably realized that few supermarkets were going to manufacture their own items, you may not have thought much about who provides the products. Typically, one of the leading branded manufacturers will also produce offerings to a store's specifications for its private label brand as a way to put idle capacity to profitable use.

At first blush, being the manufacturer who makes it easier for retailers to offer their own labels at lower prices against the manufacturer's own brand sounds like a bad option. That was my initial conclusion, too, ... until I met the CEO of a company that was then the U.S. market leader in branded garden hoses, as well as in manufacturing private-label garden hoses for anyone who wanted to be in that business. The CEO told me that making private-label hoses was more profitable than producing the branded ones. The higher private-label profitability was due to having no marketing costs and very little overhead associated with providing the garden hoses. In addition, the cost of making branded hoses was lower because of the much larger combined volume providing other efficiencies, so that branded profits were boosted, as well.

The CEO told me that his company also provided garden hoses that were branded by competitors that were not retailers. Providing these hoses, too, was very profitable.

Although competitors, wholesalers, retailers, and Wall Street knew which company made which garden hoses, relatively few consumers did. As a result, seldom was the lowest-priced item chosen by a purchaser based on knowing that it was probably identical to the highest-priced hose. It often just takes different labels and packages to change perceptions by such a large degree. If those differences are not enough, minor cosmetic changes in offerings (such as by using different shapes and colors) can "convince" purchasers of the "quality" differences so they will prefer the market leader's branded item.

When it comes to services, even more businesspeople fail to appreciate how one company can provide a service offering for a competitor's customers. The differences from what manufacturers do aren't as large as you might think. Let's look at an example.

While half-gallon containers of ice cream are a product, scooping out ice cream to put on cones or in sundaes is a service. A coffee bar might buy the ice cream in bulk from a company that also has its own ice-cream stores and add ice-cream treats to its coffee-bar offerings. Given that the coffee bar has no reputation for ice cream, it might want to use the credibility of a market leader.

In such a case, the ice cream's usual brand name might be prominently displayed. One of the coffee bar's employees could also be neatly attired in an "official" uniform of the ice cream company's retail outlets. You see this done quite often at highway rest stops where a McDonald's employee may be working as a pretzel vendor, ice cream scooper, or candy seller in an adjacent kiosk while wearing the other organization's uniform. The two "restaurants" are connected in the back, but appear to be separate to a customer.

This way of operating could work well in wintry areas where it's hard to sell enough ice cream during much of the year to pay for a retail outlet's rent and minimum staffing. By sharing overhead with the larger volume coffee bar, the specialty service operation can be profitably conducted.

Many manufacturers hire their largest service competitor to represent them in delivering specialized services that customers buy separately. In many such instances, the service supplier's vehicles, uniforms, and paperwork display the manufacturer's logo and appear to the casual observer to be from the manufacturer.

Whether it's a product, a service, or some combination of the two that your organization is providing to your competitors' customers, care must be taken to make customers feel comfortable with what they experience. Carefully test and monitor such activities to understand how joint sales and profits can be increased by making the offering more desirable to customers.

What's the key lesson? *An industry-leading organization that sincerely wants to accelerate useful innovation can be helped by providing offerings for competitors to sell to their customers so that competitors can focus more resources on faster and more effective innovation based on and copying of its most successful innovations.*

<u>Your Lesson Thirty-Three Assignments</u>

1. How could you and your stakeholders benefit because you provide competitors with offerings to sell to their customers?

2. What would have to change about your innovation practices if competitors became more effective innovators due to your organization providing offerings for competitors to sell to their customers?

3. How could you use interacting with competitors through providing them with offerings to sell to improve valuable innovation activities?

4. What could you do now to encourage making valuable innovations available sooner ... before considering the spur of competitors more quickly following in your tracks?

5. How can you prepare in advance to make any gains from providing offerings for competitors to sell to their customers even more productive for your organization, your stakeholders, and the industry?

Lesson Thirty-Four

Develop Brands and Sell Them to Competitors

"Give, and it will be given to you:
good measure, pressed down,
shaken together, and running over
will be put into your bosom.
For with the same measure that you use,
it will be measured back to you."

— Luke 6:38 (NKJV)

Many people have observed that there is often a sort of rough justice operating in the world. If you do something good for someone, someone else will sooner or later do something good for you ... with the good often coming from unexpected sources. How does that effect relate to business? Most organizations are incapable of developing a vibrant new brand for their offerings. If your organization has that skill, you have an opportunity to test the teaching of Luke 6:38 (NKJV) by selling some of your successful brands to those organizations that would make good use of them for innovation and copying purposes. Then see what happens!

A great way to develop a market faster is by creating a series of complementary brands. Each brand should provide combinations of benefits, features, design, functionality, and value that are powerfully appealing to different customers and end users.

After a brand has provided the same or similar characteristics for some time, many purchasers and end users will begin to strongly associate the brand with those characteristics. After a while, it will rarely be a good idea to make any major shifts in such characteristics... unless some major breakthrough is possible.

With a new breakthrough, you will have an opportunity to develop and sell a new, complementary brand to a competitor for the purpose of stimulating more innovation and copying. Naturally, the competitor will also be quite interested in acquiring the intellectual property to continue providing the brand and to build on any equity it has with customers and end users. It will be in your interest to be generous in supplying such intellectual property, in part because to do so will encourage more innovation and copying, and in part due to the price received for the brand with such benefits attached being higher than it would otherwise be.

If you know that you may someday want to sell a brand to encourage copying of your organization's innovations, it will also make sense to either operate such a brand from separate premises with its own dedicated staff or to totally outsource operations to organizations that will be available and eager to serve the competitor to whom you later sell the brand.

If it's not possible to create such operational independence, consider making a legal arrangement to provide either essential or hard-to-duplicate operations to your competitor after making the brand sale. Doing so will make it easier and more natural for your future innovations to migrate to the offerings of any competitors that buy your brands.

A subtle and potentially even more valuable strategy can be to make the brands that are sold so large and profitable that competitors will feel compelled to shift their existing operations into the organizational methods and facilities that are used by the acquired brand or brands. Should that result occur, the amount of innovation and copying will greatly increase.

Let me use a hypothetical example to help make these points clearer. I'll assume that Apple wants to encourage more innovation for its tablets (the iPad brand) by developing additional brands and selling these brands to competitors.

Such offerings would only be attractive if they had access to the iPad operating system and the many application programs that have been written for the iPad.

The iPad could be extended to provide a more expensive tablet with more user features and choices. An interesting approach could be to allow a user to stay in the iPad universe of applications, and to separately operate the tablet with applications from outside the iPad universe. To make this approach work, there might be two processors and two sets of memory involved. The offering might have a slightly different, more expensive look in its design and colors. Let's call this product the ultimatePad.

Below the iPad could be designed a very inexpensive tablet that would have just the most popular iPad applications and be more compact and look a little less stylish and glossy. Let's call this product the miniPad.

The ultimatePad might help attract a software-oriented competitor such as Google to enter the market, while the miniPad might help attract a consumer electronics hardware maker from Asia, especially Japan or Korea. To encourage these dual possibilities, the two brands should be operated independently of the iPad line and one another while having full access to the iPad operating system and applications.

After selling the brands, Apple could easily extend its iPad line or start new brands that would compete with the ultimatePad and the miniPad. Whatever improvements iPad made in its operating system and applications would have been licensed to its competitors who bought the brands. Consequently, any upgrades would almost immediately migrate to the other two brands, thus ensuring a high degree of copying. Advertising and shape-related features would become major points of differentiation, encouraging faster market growth and competition in forms to which the iPad could easily respond. With license fees for the software from competitors, iPad profits and cash flow would probably be higher.

Do you see the advantages for Apple? I'm sure you do.

What's the key lesson? *An industry-leading organization that sincerely wants to accelerate useful innovation can be helped by making it easier for competitors to copy what the leader does by developing competing brands that operate on a standalone basis and selling such brands to competitors with access to necessary technology and processes, so that competitors will focus more resources on faster and more effective innovation and copying of your most successful innovations ... thus setting the bar higher for what the leader will need to seek to accomplish for itself in innovation.*

Your Lesson Thirty-Four Assignments

1. How could you and your stakeholders benefit because you develop brands and sell them to competitors?

2. What would have to change about your innovation practices if competitors become more effective innovators and copiers due to your organization selling brands to competitors and providing any necessary technology and processes?

3. How could you use making it easier for competitors to succeed by selling brands to them and providing any necessary technology and processes as advantages in stimulating your future innovation activities?

4. What could you do now to encourage making valuable innovations available sooner ... before considering the spur of such

enhanced competitors more quickly following, and possibly sur-passing, your improvements?

5. How can you prepare in advance to make increasing any gains from selling brands to competitors and providing any necessary technology and processes even more productive for your organization, your stakeholders, and the industry?

Lesson Thirty-Five

Form Joint Ventures
With Competitors

Though they join forces,
the wicked will not go unpunished;
But the posterity of the righteous
will be delivered.

— Proverbs 11:21 (NKJV)

I love this proverb because it captures what I've noticed about joint ventures: They only work if the people involved care about each other and act righteously for the benefit of as many stakeholders as possible. If you want two unscrupulous competitors to disappear, hope that they will form a joint venture. The chances are good that they will damage each other enough in the process to stop being effective rivals.

Joint ventures can be very precise, delicate, and flexible ways to share knowledge, intellectual property, plans, and perspectives. Typically, a joint venture contains executives and managers from each of the venture owners.

Let me be quick to point out that a joint venture can also comprise ownership, leaders, and resources from more than just two organizations, the form that many joint ventures have often taken. Today, joint ventures are much more likely to include at least three partners ... none of whom has a larger ownership stake than any other partner. Such structures offer several potential advantages:

- In many countries, none of the venture partners can consolidate the revenues and profits (or losses) from the venture onto the parent company's profit-and-loss statement. This feature is most welcome for ventures that may be years away from earning a profit, but whose work is essential to the industry's and the partners' development.
- Skills, knowledge, and scarce resources can be drawn from at least two additional organizations for the joint venture, potentially providing for a substantial improvement in the venture's opportunities to succeed.
- If one of the partners later wants to sell or exit the venture, there are more ways that such a shift can be accommodated without eliminating a venture structure involving at least one other competitor or potential competitor as a partner.
- Management continuity is more likely to occur within the joint venture because the partners will typically take a more hands-off role in overseeing what the venture does.

Many people also don't realize that a joint venture can be established for a wide variety of narrow purposes. Naturally, if the partners want to establish a new competitor as a way to enter a market, such a broad-based purpose can be employed. Such a purpose is, however, unlikely to meet the needs of an innovative industry leader that wants to encourage copying to stimulate its own organization to be quicker to make breakthroughs. A variation on this theme can be developing joint ventures for narrower market entries, such as into market segments where the industry leader is weak or lacks skills to innovate. The geographical joint ventures between Xerox and its partners Rank (in Europe) and Fuji (in Asia), discussed most recently in Lesson Thirty, were partially designed to play such a role.

For encouraging more and faster innovation and copying, narrowly focused joint ventures are ideal ... especially ones that are directed at working on innovations that exceed what the partner that is an industry leader has already accomplished. Typically, such projects are limited in success because of not gaining enough attention from the most capable researchers in an organization. In a joint venture, by contrast, it's often possible to have a focus that perfectly fits what a research staff hopes to accomplish, having perhaps only one, two, or three major activities to work, rather than dozens.

Imagine that Boeing is looking at such an approach to joint ventures for developing new aircraft. Rather than joint venture with Airbus, something that legal and regulatory authorities would be unlikely to permit, Boeing could joint venture with suppliers to produce innovations that the suppliers would then be free to provide to Airbus, putting competitive pressure on Boeing to innovate more often and more effectively. These joint ventures might be formed around aspects of aircraft manufacture such as avionics, wings, composite structures, engines, interiors, cargo-carrying, and safety.

Consider, too, that joint ventures can focus just on research, development, operations, cost reductions, eliminating investments, distribution, customer service, or repairs (or even just fault correction). Although the list of potential joint venture structures is almost endless, in practice it can become burdensome to staff and manage too many of such joint ventures.

In some parent organizations, joint ventures won't be taken seriously. As a result, for knowledge to flow properly it's critical to have credible, visible, and expert liaisons who are influential people in the parent organizations.

Why do competitors want to be involved? In most instances, their incentives will be to access some source of competitive advantage from your organization that their organizations lack. If your organization has valuable intellectual property, that can be enough, particularly if you are not anxious to license the IP directly to competitors, but don't have such concerns about joint ventures in which you participate.

In other cases, customer access may be limited outside of a joint-venture structure. If customers are much larger and more powerful than your organization and its competitors, the biggest ones may demand an ownership stake in a joint venture as a way of limiting their costs of being supplied.

In any event, you want to be sure that your joint-venture partners bring their best capabilities to the venture. A good way to do that is by limiting any use of the know-how developed by the joint venture to the venture. Arrange matters so that partners may buy offerings from the venture, but not acquire technology licenses and other ways of circumventing the partnership.

What's the key lesson? *An industry-leading organization that sincerely wants to accelerate useful innovation can be helped by making it easier for competitors to innovate and copy by creating joint ventures with competitors that are aimed at making breakthroughs, permitting competitors to focus more resources on faster and more effective innovation and copying of your most successful breakthroughs ... thus setting the bar higher for what the industry-leading organization will need to seek to accomplish for itself in innovation.*

Your Lesson Thirty-Five Assignments

1. How could you and your stakeholders benefit because you make it easier for competitors to copy because you joint venture with them?

2. What would have to change about your innovation practices if competitors become more effective innovators and copiers due to joint venturing with them?

3. How could you use making it easier for competitors to succeed in innovating and copying by joint venturing with them as an advantage in stimulating your future innovations?

4. What could you do now to encourage making valuable innovations available sooner from your organization ... before considering the spur of such enhanced competitors more quickly accessing your knowledge, capabilities, and resources?

5. How can you prepare in advance to make any gains in increasing competitors' innovation and copying by joint venturing with them even more productive for your organization, your stakeholders, and the industry?

Lesson Thirty-Six

Sell Competitors' Offerings

"And if you sell anything to your neighbor
or buy from your neighbor's hand,
you shall not oppress one another."

— Leviticus 25:14 (NKJV)

Leviticus 25:14 (NKJV) simply tells us the obvious about applying righteous behavior to business transactions: We should treat those with whom we buy or sell fairly. Given the delicate potential nature of having such dealings with a competitor, we need to be all the more cautious to avoid either being unrighteousness in fact or appearing to have acted thusly.

In Lesson Thirty-Three, we discuss the idea of producing offerings for the competitors' customers that are branded under the competitors' name. In this lesson, we look, instead, at gaining permission from competitors to sell their offerings, regardless of how produced or provided, on a nonexclusive basis.

Some might see taking such an action as a Trojan horse, a way of pretending to help a competitor while actually harming it in some surreptitious way, much as the Greeks smuggled some men into the gift horse who later opened the gates to Troy, making possible the city's conquest. Such an approach is far from my intention.

If you aren't used to the idea of selling a competitors' offerings, think about what most supermarket chains do. In any product category, such stores will stock the leading brand or brands ... and offer their own store brand, as well. The top branded product will gain the opportunity to pay the supermarket for the best shelf space. This brand will have the highest price in the category, except perhaps for some highly specialized niche offerings (such as an organic version of something that normally isn't available in organic form).

The store won't actually manufacture its own branded product, simply purchasing what it needs from one of the branded providers or a private-label manufacturer. The store brand's packaging will be simpler and less expensive. There will be no investment needed by the store for manufacturing. No brand advertising will be used. As a result, the cost of such a product to the store is pretty small. Even with a normal profit margin, the store can afford to sell its own brands at the lowest prices in their categories.

To draw attention to the "bargain" element, the store may put a greater quantity of the offering into a package so that its offerings look bigger than the branded competition. When combined with a lower price per package, the bargain element is reinforced in the customers' minds. And, of course, the store brand will be stocked right next to the leading brand on the shelf so that consumers can't miss the alternative.

That's what you are going to do ... with only one change: You are going to be the branded competitor offering to sell the other brands through its sales force and distribution channels. Here's a potential parallel: It's as if Apple were to start selling Hewlett-Packard computers and Android cell phones in its Apple stores.

As you can imagine, the stores would have to be expanded ... or offer fewer choices. But you can be sure that the number of visitors would be enormous. Here would be a great way to investigate how Apple products compare to the best offerings of its competitors through demonstrations conducted by those ever-present Apple sales representatives who wait for customers near the front door.

Let's now assume that you provide the leading brand and have the most innovative and benefit-filled offerings. You charge the highest price in the category (or certainly no lower price than any other leading competitor).

Why would a competitor want you to sell its products? In most cases, your products benefit from better distribution and visibility than the competitor. By selling your competitors' products, there's the potential for those products to reach more customers. Because the sales and distribution costs for such sales are usually quite small for selling through your organization, it's probably a profitable activity for the competitor to sell at wholesale prices to you.

Here's an example to think about. Most small publishers know that they can gain sales outside of their home country, but they lack any way to make such sales except through online retailers. To reach bookstores and other bricks-and-mortar retailers, they need a sales force in every country. In most cases, the small publishers hire their biggest domestic competitors to handle this task for them. If the books are popular in the home country, they will probably also be popular, as well, in nations where the same language is often used. While the volume provided to the larger publisher from such activities is small, it helps such a publisher to be more effective with customers by providing more of the customers' needs. In addition, these sales are profitable because they are made through the same sales calls that are needed for the publisher's own offerings.

How will you present the competitors' offerings? The presentations will be done in a way that you and your competitor agree to do. The competitor's marketing staff will probably have ideas for how this should work. If, for instance, the competitive offering provides some advantages in certain applications or uses, such points might be emphasized. The competitor will also suggest customer pricing, probably encouraging you to sell the product at a discount to your own so that more people will consider purchasing it.

How many sales will result? It's hard to know, but the more sales you make for the competitor ... the greater the impact will be on the competitor to copy your offerings. Why? If the competitor's offerings aren't similar enough to yours, many of the people you tell about these offerings won't be interested, hurting sales and profits. More importantly, every time that your offerings are improved, the disadvantages of the competitors' offerings will become much more apparent as you talk to your current and potential customers about both your new and your competitors' old offerings. Sales of competitors' offerings in those accounts should be strongly affected during such times, creating quite a scramble by the competitor to come up with a reasonably effective version of your latest improvements.

Knowing of such virtually guaranteed copying will keep your development teams focused on staying well ahead of what competitors can immediately provide so that the innovations your organization develops will have a longer time to enjoy advantages in the marketplace. As a consequence, developing several generations of valuable improvements will probably be well underway in your organization at all times.

What's the key lesson? *An industry-leading organization that sincerely wants to accelerate its useful innovations can be helped by selling competitors' offerings that are effective copies and substitutes for its own offerings.*

Your Lesson Thirty-Six Assignments

1. How could you and your stakeholders benefit because you sell competitors' offerings that are effective copies and substitutes for your own offerings?

2. If you sell competitors' offerings that are effective copies and substitutes for your own offerings, what would have to change about your innovation priorities, budgets, processes, and practices to encourage more innovation as a result?

3. How could you use selling competitors' offerings that are effective copies and substitutes for your own offerings as an advantage in stimulating your future innovations?

4. What else could you do now to encourage making valuable innovations available much sooner from your organization ... beyond selling competitors' offerings that are effective copies and substitutes for your own offerings?

5. How can you prepare in advance to make any gains in increasing competitors' innovation and copying because of selling competitors' offerings even more productive for your organization, your stakeholders, and the industry?

Lesson Thirty-Seven

Perform Services
For Competitors

*"If anyone serves Me, let him follow Me;
and where I am,
there My servant will be also.
If anyone serves Me,
him* My *Father will honor."*

— John 12:26 (NKJV)

Serving others isn't popular in many business cultures. In fact, a business career often appeals to some people due to a desire to be served by legions of underlings. Competitors who do think in a self-aggrandizing way will certainly be interested in receiving offers from your organization to provide services.

However, someone with such a mind-set isn't likely to be thinking about performing services for competitors. Jesus set the example in this regard at the Last Supper, as He stopped to wash His disciples' feet. We should do no less for our competitors.

Hiring your organization to provide services usually indicates, in part, a strong preference for your ways of doing business. Such relationships help employees in both companies understand how the other one works. Absent contractual limitations, workers in both organizations are more likely to seek jobs in the other one ... further increasing the amount of copying of what your organization does.

The best way to begin seeking to provide services for competitors is by identifying the important activities that competitors do most poorly for themselves. Then, first offer your services in such activities.

The effect will be to greatly lift competitors' effectiveness by either reducing or eliminating inefficiencies in their organizations and permitting competitors to focus on competing in just a few activities where they are most effective.

Many businesspeople would see offering such services as the equivalent of insanity. They were taught that businesses should seek to develop long-lasting advantages versus competitors that amount to moats filled with alligators permanently protecting their competitive position.

Such thinking is out-of-date, if it ever did apply. Instead, your company can only expect to gain lasting competitive advantages through leading in activities such as continuing business model innovation and supplying new generations of much enhanced offerings that customers and end users crave.

A helpful analogy to consider can be found in comparing the German and French military strategies during the opening days of World War II. World War I had been a particularly deadly conflict, as millions of poorly protected men unsuccessfully launched themselves against zeroed-in artillery and machine gun nests through barbed wire across mine-filled land. The trenches from which such attacks were launched went continuously from the Mediterranean to the English Channel.

Neither the Germans nor the French wanted to repeat such a debacle. The German military strategists decided that speed and mobility were of the essence, seeking to strike and move forward quickly before new defenses could solidify. Think of this as being like going where a larger, stronger opponent isn't looking.

The French had a different idea: Create a bulwark so strong that it could not be successfully attacked. They built the Maginot Line of fortresses in the northern part of their country and were prepared to make any Germans pay who tried to penetrate these defenses.

As history revealed, the Germans had the better strategy for that phase of the war. They simply attacked where there was no Maginot Line and then circled around behind it, after noting that the fortifications had virtually no ability to survive an attack from the rear.

Similarly today, some businesses imagine that they can build operating fortifications that will insulate them from whatever the enemy tries head on. They are bound to be outmaneuvered.

An example can be found in Borders bookstores and record shops' handling of online sales. With many prime retail locations contractually required to exclude its competitors, the chain felt that it would survive and thrive as long as shoppers still chose to come to shopping malls. That thinking continued until it was announced in 2011 that that Borders would be liquidated in bankruptcy.

The company's leaders had miscalculated. Today, a high percentage of books and an even higher percentage of recorded music are sold as electronic downloads. A prime mall location is no advantage for competing in such an environment.

As the trend emerged, Borders decided it wanted to avoid the expenses and difficulties of electronic marketing and distribution. Borders hired Amazon.com to provide fulfillment for its online orders. This move helped Amazon.com gain more customers and lower its costs, while keeping Borders from focusing on this most important competitive arena.

Think of this strategy in terms of judo. That martial art requires a competitor to use the opponent's size and strength as resources. That's exactly what Amazon.com did in providing such services for Borders' customers.

Amazon.com's purpose may have been to drive Borders out of the electronic business, rather than to encourage copying ... as we are seeking to do. There's no way to know. If Amazon.com's objective had been to make Borders a stronger copier, the online retailer should have, instead, provided services that made Borders a stronger competitor for electronic distribution of its own offerings. With the added credibility of Borders' participation, the electronic distribution method would have grown faster. Pushed by competition from Borders, Amazon.com would have undoubtedly improved its own offerings faster and more effectively, as well.

As the Borders example teaches, you should also seek to supply services that will provide new strategic options for competitors and you, as well as helping competitors to overcome operating weaknesses. When you can accomplish both goals by providing services to competitors, you will be most efficient in stimulating more effective competitive innovation and copying.

Why? When competitors realize that you will protect them from strategic mistakes, as well as help them to overcome operating weaknesses, they will commit greater resources to copying and trying to "one-up" your successes. As they become better at doing both activities, you'll find that your future innovations will need to be more fundamental and valuable ... stirring your organization to feel the need to be more innovative.

While it may seem as though you are giving away too much by providing such help through supplying services, in most cases your expertise will grow and your costs will decline as a result. Consequently, your competitive advantages can potentially increase by becoming more skilled in these activities.

What's the key lesson? *An industry-leading organization that sincerely wants to accelerate useful innovation can be helped by providing services to competitors that help cure their strategic mistakes and weak operations so that the competitors can become faster and more effective copiers of and improvers on the leader's most successful innovations.*

Your Lesson Thirty-Seven Assignments

1. How could you and your stakeholders benefit because you perform key activities for competitors so that they quickly become more effective in the areas where their performance now is the weakest?

2. What would have to change about your innovation practices if competitors became more effective innovators and copiers due to your organization providing them with essential services?

3. How could you use interacting with competitors through providing services to improve valuable innovation?

4. What could you do now to encourage making valuable innovations available sooner ... before considering the spur of competitors more quickly responding to your improved offerings?

5. How can you prepare in advance to make any gains from providing services for competitors even more productive for your organization, your stakeholders, and the industry?

Lesson Thirty-Eight

Train Competitors' Employees

But at midnight Paul and Silas were
praying and singing hymns to God,
and the prisoners were listening to them.

Suddenly there was a great earthquake,
so that the foundations
of the prison were shaken;
and immediately all the doors were opened
and everyone's chains were loosed.

And the keeper of the prison,
awaking from sleep
and seeing the prison doors open,
supposing the prisoners had fled,
drew his sword and
was about to kill himself.

But Paul called with a loud voice, saying,
"Do yourself no harm, for we are all here."

Then he called for a light, ran in, and
fell down trembling
before Paul and Silas.

And he brought them out and said,
"Sirs, what must I do to be saved?"

So they said, "Believe on
the Lord Jesus Christ,
and you will be saved,
you and your household."

Then they spoke the word of the Lord
to him and to all who were in his house.
And he took them the same hour
of the night and washed their *stripes.*

And immediately he and
all his family *were baptized.*

Now when he had brought them
into his house, he set food before them;
and he rejoiced, having believed in God
with all his household.

— Acts 16:25-34 (NKJV)

For the relatively few organizations that are likely to want to provide services to competitors, training is the service they are least likely to be willing to provide. Why? Training can narrow the gap between their organization and its competitors faster than many other steps described in this book.

In thinking about this option, it's instructive to study the example of the Apostle Paul in Acts 16:25-34 (NKJV). Through either natural or supernatural means, all of the prisoners were freed of their chains and could have escaped. Yet none did. The jailer, knowing that the penalty for losing a prisoner was death, prepared to kill himself. Paul quickly intervened so that the jailer did not do so. This unexpected set of events made the jailer decide that he wanted to learn about Paul's faith. Soon, the jailer and his family were saved and baptized, turning someone who had been an oppressor into a brother heading a family in Christ. Paul appears to have made similar inroads with his guards in Rome, spreading the Gospel there.

You cannot train someone without creating a lasting bond and forever changing how that person sees the world. That's the opportunity that this lesson explores.

My sense is that very few, if any, employers have ever considered providing valuable training for competitors. However, I have seen several instances of such training being supplied. The Malcolm Baldrige National Quality Award requires winners to provide free training to all those who want it. Thus, any competitors may come and learn. And they certainly do. I have attended such trainings with clients who were from competing organizations. As you can well imagine, the teaching firm didn't reveal its greatest secrets, but important lessons were clearly shared.

I believe that highly successful organizations should provide such training due to the many advantages they and their stakeholders will gain. Here are seven of the more important reasons why I come to this conclusion:

1. *Such training is a great way to find out how well you are doing important activities.* If competitors show no interest in coming to your training, that circumstance suggests that competitors feel as if they have little, if anything, to gain from what you know how to do. By extension, if a competitor flocks to some kinds of your training and is much less interested in other areas, you can get a sense of where you are probably ahead of and behind that competitor. In addition, any questions or comments that are made during the training sessions will be highly useful for appreciating more about differences in existing practices among competitors.

2. *Such training is a necessary step for improving industry stand-ards and upgrading any equipment that you are designing or sup-plying for competitors.* Much of the training for producing or servicing an offering will necessarily relate to using such equipment. In the process of explaining and demonstrating how your organization uses the equipment, you will elicit ob-servations that disagree with what your organization has con-cluded. While sharing what you know, you are highly likely to learn about problems that are harming industry develop-ment, increasing costs unnecessarily, and causing needless in-vestments. Of potentially greater import will be reactions that suggest superior methods competitors have developed to ac-complish outstanding results at the same or with less cost and investment.

3. *Such training provides opportunities to upgrade the problem-solving skills and methods of your competitors so that they will be able to spur your organization to innovate more.* A good exam-ple comes in creating complementary 2,000 percent solutions. A mere copycat organization will be able to follow much of what you do, but without understanding the reasoning behind why you do it there may be shortchanging of important steps ... such as placing an equal emphasis on helping stakeholders to prosper. When such a misunderstanding happens, competi-tors will take harmful actions without meaning to do so. If, in-stead, you can teach competitors advanced methods that you haven't yet mastered, your progress may be accelerated by study-ing what they do and their results.

4. *Providing such training is highly likely to encourage some com-petitors to also offer training that your employees can take.* Ego is a funny thing. Many people treasure recognition and applause so much that they will reveal valuable information in a public setting that should be kept private. It will gall at least some of

your competitors that everyone in the industry so highly values what you do in training. These competitors will want to outdo what you are providing. That desire will spur some of them to improve both in base performance and in how well they train others to perform the same activities. As a result, you will gain opportunities to learn and to improve that you would not have otherwise enjoyed.

5. *The most talented of competitors' employees will gain an opportunity to appreciate any advantages that working for your organization might provide to them ... helping to attract more high-potential people to work for your organization.* Many people who are very able want to work with just the best talent in the most outstanding organizations, so that they can learn more and advance faster. Since most companies disparage competitor organizations, many employees never realize that they would do better by changing employers.

6. *Knowing that making a major innovation may provide the opportunity to gain recognition and to teach others outside the organization will encourage your employees and suppliers to find more of such improvements.* As an organization becomes larger and more successful, each person who isn't near the top of the leadership feels smaller and smaller ... and less and less significant. However, gaining the applause of other organizations is ever more satisfying to such individuals. The opportunity to provide training about one's own innovations gives you a major new motivational tool for those who crave more opportunities for recognition.

7. *Developing such training will improve how effectively you train your own new employees.* By learning from training larger numbers of people who don't have to be as accepting of any weaknesses in your training methods, your own new hires and

transferred employees will get off to a better and faster start in their work.

If you agree that this approach of training competitors' employees makes sense, let me share some principles to employ in such training.

- Start by providing training in the activities where your competitors probably know the least so that they will more quickly perceive the advantages of taking such courses.
- Next, add training in the areas that seem to account for the biggest amounts of competitive advantage for your organization. These courses should draw well.
- After that, ask course graduates to describe what new courses they would like you to offer.
- Include some of your top operating people when providing such training so that the information will seem livelier and be more up-to-date, and your people can observe competitors' reactions for themselves.
- Let journalists and students attend, as well, so that the information has a better chance of being learned by potential competitors who might start making offerings.
- Provide staff and budget help for competitors who want to launch their own public training programs covering the same and similar subjects.
- Continually estimate the gaps between your performance and that of major competitors in the most important activities to see how effective your training has been in speeding up competitors' innovating and copying and your own organization's innovations.
- Forecast when competitors will reach various performance levels so that internal innovation targets can be set aggressively enough to provide an accelerated rate of performance enhancement for stakeholders versus each competitor.

What's the key lesson? *An industry-leading organization that sincerely wants to accelerate useful innovation can gain many advantages by continually training competitors in how to be more effective in the most important activities.*

Your Lesson Thirty-Eight Assignments

1. How could you and your stakeholders benefit if competitors quickly become more effective in the areas where their performances now are the weakest?

2. What would have to change about your innovation practices if competitors were trained to quickly duplicate everything that you have learned to accomplish?

3. How could you use interacting with competitors in training sessions to improve valuable innovation?

4. What could you do now to encourage making valuable innovations available sooner ... before considering the spur of competitors quickly learning what you know?

5. How can you prepare in advance to make any gains from training competitors even more productive for your organization, your stakeholders, and the industry?

Lesson Thirty-Nine

Acquire, Improve, and Sell Competitors

Now Joseph had been taken down to Egypt.
And Potiphar, an officer of Pharaoh,
captain of the guard, an Egyptian,
bought him from the Ishmaelites
who had taken him down there.

— Genesis 39:1 (NKJV)

Because of their jealousy, Joseph's brothers sold him into slavery, afterwards pretending to their father that he had been killed. Potiphar later purchased Joseph. Since the Lord was with him, Joseph did well for Potiphar, and he was put over the household. All was well until Potiphar's wife falsely accused Joseph of a serious sexual offense. Consequently, Joseph was thrown into prison, but he also did well in this new environment. Later, Joseph had a chance to help Pharaoh by interpreting a dream leading to his becoming second in command of Egypt.

Whenever I think about the possibilities of acquiring a competitor, improving the company, and then selling it, Joseph comes to mind as an example of such a valuable transformation. Of course, it was God's hand that made it possible. Keep that lesson in mind. If you seek to expand God's Kingdom by following this example, pray that His hand will be with you, as well.

Acquiring competitors is almost always successful. Why? Costs can be lowered by eliminating redundancies (such has having two headquarters, extra plants or operating centers, two sales forces, and duplicative marketing expenses). In addition, the remaining staff and facilities can be operated more efficiently by being thoughtfully combined with what you do, further reducing costs and investments. In addition, each organization has some knowledge and strengths that can be shared with the other one ... creating the opportunity for still more efficiencies than either organization could conceive of by itself. Some new customers are attracted by the opportunity to work with the more accomplished, combined company. Finally, price competition is probably somewhat reduced so that profit contribution could increase, enabling more funding for innovation.

Most companies that acquire competitors don't realize there's an even more desirable strategy available: Improve the acquired organization and then sell it. In the process, a more effective competitor can be created that will have gained intimate knowledge of what your organization does well and what it does poorly. In the process, you can transfer personnel and assets so that the new organization is in a better position to improve on and copy what you do now ... and will do in the future.

There's also a bit of extra icing on such a strategic cake: When the competitor is sold, the price received will probably be much greater than the price paid ... providing a near-term bonus in profits and cash flow for all this hard work and launching of a more effective competitor. Such new finances can fund still more innovation.

While I can't point to a major company that has continually engaged in such a strategy, there's a somewhat analogous situation within the Coca-Cola bottling network that we can consider. Let's look at that experience.

Because Coca-Cola was founded and grew to be large long before Pepsi-Cola did, some Coca-Cola bottlers were larger and had been in business longer than their Pepsi counterparts. Despite these potential advantages, many of the Coca-Cola bottlers were still small, family-run enterprises. By the 1980s, many such organizations were headed by someone who was a third-generation descendant of the founders. With large assured profits and solid cash flow, many owners were more interested in picking out their new yachts than in improving operations and selling more soft drinks.

Faced with a surging Pepsi-Cola that successfully used promotional discounting in combination with taste-test results showing most people preferred Pepsi, Coca-Cola needed to strengthen its bottler network. To do so, the parent organization began purchasing its weakest bottlers, making necessary investments, upgrading management teams, and encouraging greater local marketing efforts.

To pay for the investments, Coca-Cola would eventually sell the bottlers to new owners (either privately or through a public stock offering). The increased profits from these divestitures boosted Coca-Cola's share price. The sales yielded gains so substantial that they more than repaid the operating investments that were made.

More significantly, Coca-Cola developed substantial expertise in improving bottling and distribution operations so that the amount of time required for making the necessary improvements became quite brief.

In applying such a strategy for improving competitors to make them more effective in innovating and copying what you do, I suggest that you engage in a strategy that's somewhat different from what Coca-Cola did. Here are six ideas for your consideration:

1. Instead of acquiring the weakest competitors to begin, start by acquiring your strongest competitor. Taking such an action first reduces any legal risk that government laws or regulations will stop the transaction. In addition, you will gain the most benefit in encouraging innovation and copying by strengthening your most effective competitor.

2. Finish improving and divesting your strongest competitor before acquiring any other competitors. Taking such an action reduces any legal risk that government laws or regulations will stop such future transactions. Further, you will know a great deal more about how to improve other competitors after making the most out of the combined knowledge and operations of you and your strongest competitor.

3. When divesting the first acquired competitor, don't seek to replicate the size and structure of the prior organization. Instead, create a more formidable competitor that will have an easier time innovating and copying you and being effective in taking away customers during times when you lose your innovation advantages. Ideally, such an organization will include many people from your existing organization who are well equipped to copy and improve on your current and future innovations.

4. As the second acquisition, seek the next-most effective competitor and proceed as with the first to make improvements, creating a more powerful competitor, and selling a reconfigured business.

5. Continue sequentially through the industry, one competitor at a time, until you are working on such small organizations that you can afford the staff time and the finances needed to improve more than one entity simultaneously.

6. Don't wait to for the increased competitive effectiveness you are creating to become a knife beginning to cut your organization's throat before you start improving your innovation. Instead, simultaneously with the first acquisition begin upgrading your organization's innovation capabilities. In making upgrades to your own capabilities for innovation, include all the useful practices that your acquired competitors teach you.

What's the key lesson? *An industry-leading organization that sincerely wants to accelerate useful innovation can be helped by acquiring* competitors, *improving them, and then selling the organizations so that competitors can focus more resources on faster and more effective innovation and copying of the leader's most successful breakthroughs ... thus setting the bar higher for what the leader organization will need to seek to accomplish for itself in innovation.*

Your Lesson Thirty-Nine Assignments

1. How could you and your stakeholders benefit because you acquire, improve, and then sell competitors?

2. What would have to change about your innovation practices if competitors become more effective innovators due to your organization acquiring, improving, and selling them?

3. How could you use interacting with competitors through acquiring, improving, and selling them to improve your own valuable innovations?

4. What could you do now to encourage making valuable innovations available sooner ... before considering the spur of such enhanced competitors being more effective in innovation and copying?

5. How can you prepare in advance to make any gains from acquiring, improving, and selling competitors even more productive for your organization, your stakeholders, and the industry?

Lesson Forty

Make Competitors Aware Of the Profit Bonanza Available from Copying

"The blind see and the lame walk;
the lepers are cleansed and the deaf hear;
the dead are raised up and
the poor have the gospel preached to them."

— Matthew 11:5 (NKJV)

Because the Old Testament contains prophecies about the Messiah that include these miraculous deeds occurring, Jesus chose to share them in response to John the Baptist's inquiry if He was the Messiah. Notice that this proof included preaching the Gospel message, as well as deeds consistent with that message being true. Similarly, business leaders need to help competitors appreciate the profit potential of innovative copying by saying so, as well as by demonstrating the fact.

This lesson is also informed by *Steve Jobs*, by Walter Isaacson. As I read the book, I was fascinated by how fast Apple's innovations attracted competitors who made their own innovations. For example, Microsoft became enamored of the GUI (Graphic User Interface — clicking on an icon with a mouse, rather than typing in a command)

and produced Windows to compete with Apple's Macintosh operating system in the IBM Personal Computer (PC) world.

In the case of Microsoft, Apple invited the software maker to write application programs, such as Word and Excel. Seeing how the GUI attracted purchasers to the Macintosh who normally wouldn't have considered purchasing from a company like Apple made Microsoft curious. By charging a great deal for its equipment and software, Apple also created a price umbrella that made it potentially very profitable for copiers who could produce reasonably good alternatives. Aware that there would be a great amount of competition among PC makers (where the standard was open for copying from the beginning), Microsoft shrewdly appreciated that rapidly falling PC hardware prices would allow Microsoft to charge ever more for its Windows operating system and its application programs while still undercutting what Apple charged for Macintosh computers and related software.

Thinking back to that period in computer history, I also recall the experiences of Verbatim Corporation, then the leader in producing floppy disks, a popular medium used for portable electronic storage at the time. Verbatim was one of the first companies to make reliable 5 1/4 inch floppy disks. In doing so, Verbatim developed its own electronic media from which it cut out the "cookies" that went into the floppy-disk holders. Most of its competitors relied on external media suppliers such as 3M, which also supplied branded floppy disks. 3M and the other suppliers charged a great deal for their media, so anyone who could make their own could earn an enormous profit.

Verbatim was a relatively small technology company at the time, and the stock market multiples for such firms were fairly low. As a result, the firm was financially constrained from trying to gain too much market share by what it was willing to borrow ... which wasn't very much. In addition, Verbatim bought its media-making machines from a custom manufacturer in Europe that had a large backlog. Decisions to buy equipment made in 1981 determined how much media could be made in 1983. When the market exploded, it exceeded everyone's expectations and supplies were limited.

As a result, Verbatim knew that people would buy the floppy disks they needed from someone. So the company followed a profit-optimizing strategy of charging for its disks as if it were purchasing media from 3M. Consequently, the publicly traded firm enjoyed an enormous profit margin. Current and potential competitors took note, and dozens of companies entered the market with purchased media that copied Verbatim's offerings.

The next round of floppy-disk innovation was the plastic-cased 3 1/2 inch disk. All competitors prepared for a race to reach the market first. Not knowing how the floppy drives would work, they could only assume what might be needed. When the first drives became available, Verbatim's and others' preparatory media flopped, and the race to supply the market was eventually won by others. Long-standing orders for purchasing media-making equipment had been cancelled, and the person who kept the media line running left to work for a competitor. As a result, Verbatim lost its competitive advantage during this wave of innovation and was ultimately purchased by Eastman Kodak.

As you can see from these two examples, it's much easier to attract copying competitors with high prices and rich profit margins than it is to stay ahead of them in innovation. In both the Apple and the Verbatim examples, key employees were lost who were essential to maintaining competitiveness and producing innovations.

Before embarking on the strategy of letting competitors know that they can earn an unusually large profit by copying and competing with you, be sure that you can sustain whatever competitive advantage you rely on and know how to create the next rounds of needed innovations well in advance of your copying competitors. Otherwise, you would do well to charge less and not encourage quite so much copying.

Let me describe seven circumstances under which this strategy of encouraging copying by providing the opportunity to earn profit bonanzas works well:

1. Competitors are likely to copy and to be innovative, but they are unlikely to make a major challenge for industry leadership through improvements or being able to provide the bulk of the market's needs.
2. You can sustain or improve your advantages in retaining the most highly talented and effective people in the industry.
3. Your future innovations will occur more rapidly than competitors so that you will have periods with no copying of such innovations before sales are affected by competitors.
4. Major innovations will occur fairly frequently and are more predictable in what must be done than is typically the case in other industries.
5. Innovation is mostly under your own control rather than being dependent on what others do, enabling you to secure lead-time advantages over current and potential competitors.
6. You cannot hope to supply all the increased demand stimulated by the innovations.
7. Your colleagues have a healthy fear of being overtaken by copying competitors and prefer to respond to such challenges with increased innovation.

What's the key lesson? *An industry-leading organization that sincerely wants to accelerate its useful innovations can be helped under certain circumstances by letting competitors know about the opportunity to enjoy a profit bonanza by copying its offerings and processes.*

Your Lesson Forty Assignments

1. How could you and your stakeholders benefit because you let competitors know about the opportunity to enjoy a profit bo-

nanza by copying you and adding innovations, providing an incentive for competitors to very rapidly follow your big successes in this regard?

2. What would have to change about your innovation priorities, budgets, processes, and practices if competitors become more effective copiers of your offerings after you let them know about the opportunity to enjoy a profit bonanza from copying you?

3. How could you use developing superior solutions and letting competitors know about the opportunity to enjoy a profit bonanza by copying you as an advantage in stimulating your future innovations?

4. What could you do now to encourage making valuable innovations available much sooner from your organization ... beyond what letting competitors know about the opportunity to enjoy a profit bonanza by copying you will provide?

5. How can you prepare in advance to make any gains in increasing competitors' innovation and copying even more productive for your organization, your stakeholders, and the industry?

Lesson Forty-One

Encourage Syndicated Research

Then it happened, when Ahab saw Elijah,
that Ahab said to him,
"Is that you, O troubler of Israel?"

And he answered,
"I have not troubled Israel,
but you and your father's house have,
in that you have forsaken
the commandments of the LORD and
have followed the Baals.
Now therefore, send and gather all Israel
to me on Mount Carmel,
the four hundred and fifty prophets of Baal,
and the four hundred prophets of Asherah,
who eat at Jezebel's table."

— 1 Kings 18:17-19 (NKJV)

After the evil-doing King Ahab followed Elijah's directions in 1 Kings 18:17-19 (NKJV), Elijah challenged the prophets of Baal to use supernatural fire to burn a sacrificed bull. When they could not do so, Elijah mocked them and then successfully called on God to burn a second sacrificial bull. I like to think of this occasion as an example of how objective research can provide what the truth is, even when the truth relates to something unseen, such as what is in the supernatural realm. Let's now turn our attention to opportunities today to make similar gains in expanding God's Kingdom.

What do I mean by "syndicated research?" The term simply refers to any kind of research paid for by more than one sponsor and the results can likewise be used by each sponsor. Typically, the organization that conducts the research is independent of any of the sponsors. A well-known example of such research in the United States can be found in the Nielsen ratings that track how many people watch various television programs. The Nielsen organization does the measuring, and programmers and advertisers subscribe to learn what viewers watch.

Syndicated research offers both advantages and disadvantages compared to proprietary research for encouraging your company's innovation. Let's start with the advantages:

- Reduced cost for each sponsor to obtain the results
- Ability to afford doing more research
- Reduced risk of confusing the market by applying conflicting data that could be harmful to consumption of offerings
- Enhanced ability to gain an objective view of performance versus competitors
- Increased ability to attract scarce resources and essential people to conduct the research
- Greater credibility of results
- Improved analysis based on probing by many sponsors

The disadvantages are fewer, but important:

- Competitors see the same information as you do for much of what is produced, making it harder for any competitors to gain a proprietary advantage.
- Such research is often more general than an individual organization would prefer.

- Due to needing to satisfy many sponsors, the research usually takes longer to conduct and is less timely.
- Access to syndicated research makes it easier for new companies to enter an industry and to sustain a presence in it.

With our intent of encouraging innovation and copying by competitors, you can see that even the disadvantages demonstrate that syndicated research is an important opportunity for increasing the likelihood that all competitors will be aware of the same information and will probably emphasize the same kinds of factors and improvements with new and existing offerings.

In the context of this lesson, there are many kinds of research that might be syndicated. Here are a few of the most important kinds:

- Offering performance measurements (Such research is good for learning end-user experiences with offerings, both good and bad; a well-known example in the United States can be found in the J.D. Power and Associates surveys to ascertain and rank vehicle and service quality.)
- Offering usage patterns (Such research can identify emerging applications and needs that require more specialized attention and offerings.)
- Advertising awareness (Show which advertisements succeed in gaining attention and creating a memory.)
- Offering image (Identify how customers and end users perceive who should use various offerings and when the offerings should be used.)
- Offering availability (Identify where offerings can be obtained and in what varieties and types.)
- Initial quality (Expose flaws that offerings and services contain when first received.)
- Long-term quality (Identify flaws that reveal themselves as time passes.)

- Behavioral patterns (Show characteristics of how purchasers and end users interact with offerings.)
- Identifying unsolved problems (Make behavioral observations and measurements to notice ways that the value of offerings can be enhanced.)
- Estimating offering demand (Describe potential new offerings and elicit purchase intentions.)
- Purchase plans (Find out when current and potential customers will most likely make their next purchases and what they will be.)
- Cross-elasticity measurements (Ask purchasers and end users how they make trade-offs among functional substitutes.)
- Physical testing for durability and reliability
- Technological development

In addition, an industry leader should be aware that its own actions can have a large impact on the availability of such syndicated research. For example, when such information is needed, an industry leader could ask potential suppliers to canvass competitors to determine their interest in joining a syndicated project, rather than automatically commissioning a proprietary project. An industry leader could also make public comments about the value to customers and end users of there being more syndicated research done by the industry. In such cases, customers and users are more likely to push competitors to sponsor syndicated research.

What's the key lesson? *An industry-leading organization that sincerely wants to accelerate useful innovation can be helped by making it easy for competitors to learn what the leader does on the same schedule by encouraging and participating in syndicated research, so that competitors will focus more resources on faster and more effective innovation and copying of the leader's most successful breakthroughs ... thus setting the bar higher for what the leader organization will need to seek to accomplish for itself in innovation.*

Your Lesson Forty-One Assignments

1. How could you and your stakeholders benefit because you make it easy for competitors to sponsor syndicated research?

2. What would have to change about your innovation practices if competitors become more effective innovators and copiers due to your organization making it easy to sponsor syndicated research?

3. How could you use making it easy to participate in syndicated research to improve your own valuable innovations?

4. What could you do now to encourage making valuable innovations available sooner ... before considering the spur of such enhanced competitors more quickly following what you focus on?

5. How can you prepare in advance to make any gains from making it easy for competitors to participate in syndicated research even more productive for your organization, your stakeholders, and the industry?

Lesson Forty-Two

Found
Public-Research Institutes

Therefore he reasoned in the synagogue
with the Jews and with the Gentile worshipers,
and in the marketplace daily
with those who happened to be there.

— Acts 17:17 (NKJV)

When the Apostle Paul came to Athens, he found an opportunity to teach in a new way by addressing those who liked to discuss new ideas in the streets. So he added doing that to his daily activities, supplementing what he taught in the synagogue. In the streets, Paul eventually attracted enough interest to be taken to the Areopagus, the highest judicial and legislative council in Athens. Sharing the Gospel there was an ancient equivalent of many activities conducted by today's public-research institutes that seek to improve government policies.

What do I mean by "public-research institutes" as the term is applied to innovations in a modern industry? These are typically non-profit organizations that develop technology and license it to anyone willing to pay a standard royalty either as a percentage of sales or per unit produced. Such organizations are typically more focused on commercial applications than are universities. In addition, these organizations usually concentrate on certain aspects of a single industry. Thus, such a medical institute might focus on developing treatments for just certain aspects of a given disease (such as the Dana-Farber Cancer Institute does in seeking cures for certain types of cancer and related diseases).

Such institutes are quite a blessing for circumstances where the potential of technology exceeds the public and industry resources available to develop and apply the technology. I believe that such institutes offer greatest value for innovation in smaller industries for companies operating in lesser developed countries. Through applying the research that such institutes conduct, small companies may be able to innovate rather than merely rely on partially copying what larger, more established firms do.

With so many countries seeking to set up new export industries or to expand existing ones, such institutes can be in a good position to also receive support from public universities in a given country, as well as direct grants from one or more local governments.

In many cases, private companies are given preferred access to new technology from such institutes in exchange for paying substantial annual dues.

Those who work for such institutes often go on to become highly valuable research personnel for private companies.

As with syndicated market research, there are a number of substantial benefits from sharing the costs of such research and development of technology as compared to simply doing proprietary development. Those benefits include:

- Reduced cost for each sponsor to obtain the results
- Ability to afford conducting more research
- Less reduction in reported earnings during lengthy technology-development projects
- Decreased risk of providing ineffective or unsafe technology due to greater external scrutiny

- Enhanced ability to gain an objective view of a company's internal technology competence
- Increased ability to attract scarce resources and essential people to conduct the research
- Greater credibility of results
- Improved analysis based on probing by many sponsors

The disadvantages are fewer, but important:

- Competitors see the same information you do for much of what is produced, making it harder for a competitor to gain a proprietary advantage.
- Such research is often more general than an individual organization would prefer for establishing a specific offering.
- Due to potentially needing to satisfy many sponsors, the research may take longer to conduct.
- Public research institutes make it easier to enter an industry and to sustain a presence in it.

You can see that even these disadvantages can advance innovation and copying by increasing the likelihood that all competitors are aware of the same technical information and are probably emphasizing some of the same kinds of improvements with new and existing offerings.

The types of technology that should be conducted by such institutes vary from industry to industry. In most cases, the projects should be designed to generate breakthroughs rather than incremental improvements, especially breakthroughs that will accelerate market expansion and greatly reduce costs and investments for all stakeholders.

As with syndicated research, the industry leader's actions have a large impact on the potential to establish such institutes and to affect the directions that their research takes. In fact, it's highly unlikely that an institute will be founded without the enthusiastic support of the industry leader.

These influences by the industry leader are all quite understandable. After all, much of the potential funding to make such an institute effective will have to come from the industry leader. In addition, without input concerning research plans from the industry leader, many others will be reluctant to add their financial resources and talent.

You may be wondering why I suggested founding research institutes in the plural. That's because the research directors of such organizations often have narrow expertise and interests. In addition, such organizations can sometimes be ineffective. With competition from other public-research institutes, such ineffectiveness is somewhat more likely to be avoided for the industry.

Notice that since there will still be substantial work required to apply any new technology, due to its greater size and experience in innovation the industry leader can still expect to enjoy a lead-time advantage in bringing new offerings to market, as well as in being able to produce better offerings. In fact, competitors may wait until the market leader's new offering is out before finalizing their own offerings.

What's the key lesson? *An industry-leading organization that sincerely wants to accelerate useful innovation can be helped by making it easier for competitors to learn on the same schedule what the leader does about advanced technology that's too expensive for any individual company to afford to develop by encouraging and participating in public-research institutes, so that competitors will focus more resources on faster and more effective innovation and copying of the leader's most successful innovations ... thus setting the bar higher for what the leader organization will need to seek to accomplish for itself in innovation.*

Your Lesson Forty-Two Assignments

1. How could you and your stakeholders benefit because you make it easier for competitors to access advanced technology by founding public-research institutes?

2. What would have to change about your innovation practices if competitors become more effective innovators and copiers due to your organization making it easier for competitors to access advanced technology by founding public-research institutes?

3. How could you use making it easier for competitors to access advanced technology by founding public-research institutes to improve your own valuable innovations?

4. What could you do now to encourage making valuable innovations available sooner ... before considering the spur of such enhanced competitors becoming more effective?

5. How can you prepare in advance to make any gains from making it easier for competitors to access advanced technology by founding public-research institutes even more productive for your organization, your stakeholders, and the industry?

Lesson Forty-Three

Sponsor University-Research Programs

Then Barnabas departed for Tarsus to seek Saul.
And when he had found him,
he brought him to Antioch.
So it was that for a whole year
they assembled with the church and
taught a great many people.
And the disciples were first called
Christians in Antioch.

— Acts 11:25-26 (NKJV)

After the Holy Spirit descended on the believers in Jerusalem, many Jews began to believe in the Gospel. These conversions ultimately triggered a backlash that included the martyrdom of Stephen. After that, believers scattered. Reports soon indicated that Gentiles, as well, were receiving the faith. Barnabas was dispatched to Antioch to see what was happening, and his sharing of the Gospel there was well received. Wanting to do more, Barnabas asked Paul to join him. Together, they spent a year developing the Gospel message to share with Gentiles.

To me, this experience in Antioch was much like commissioning a university investigator to check some development opportunities and then to establish an ongoing research program that includes teaching undergraduate and graduate students. Let's look at how such an activity can be valuable for improving innovation and copying.

In lessons thirty-eight and forty-two, we explored the ideas of encouraging copying by training competitors' employees and by founding public-research institutes. This present lesson is complementary to those activities and expands the potential for innovation and copying in more fundamental ways.

People are often creatures of their not-very-often-considered habits. I am often reminded of that when I meet bright, young MBA graduates who did well with applying quantitative analyses while in business school. They often make very predictable errors in applying their learning without realizing that they are doing so.

When I am first asked to work with an organization, I make it a practice to meet as many people there as possible in order to become acquainted with and to start understanding the ways that they see their circumstances. When compiling the list of whom to meet, I always ask if there are any bright people who are often relied on for analytical work. Invariably one or two will be identified.

In the course of our conversations, I expect that the analysts will have only considered standard analyses and will have sometimes assumed the conclusion by forcing the data to fit one or more of the models usually taught in business schools. As a result, the analysts may have totally missed what the data are demonstrating. Since most executives and managers have, at best, modest quantitative analytical skills, whatever perspective the analysts have applied will be the controlling one for the organization.

One of my favorite examples of this comes in exploring elasticity of demand. Microeconomics favors a certain definition of elasticity. Those who know that definition may take pride in not using any other data or ratios to learn how demand might be shifted. As a consequence, such analysts may not look at anything but the one definition, one that usually isn't very revealing for strategic decisions.

My point is that formal education within a specialty, especially at the graduate level, can easily become a set of blinders that overly focus attention on a few areas. Naturally, such a set of blinders becomes a marvelous way to encourage copying of the approach your organization takes to innovation in offerings, business models, and strategy.

Establishing such university programs as a sponsor typically allows an organization to put a large stamp on what is taught by influencing what educational purposes are served, having a say in who is selected to teach, and providing some students with access to your organization's facilities and knowledge. As a result, students who graduate from the program will be deeply imbued with the perspectives you would like to foster.

However, don't stop at being the establishing sponsor. Encourage your competitors to do the same. Such involvement usually allows them to see research sooner, as well as to have more access to graduates of any programs related to the research.

If, in addition, you make it a practice to do some of your entry-level hiring from among a program's top graduates, you will probably create an enormous incentive to think like your organization does and to encourage students to curry favor with your organization before graduating. Of course, many of the graduates of such programs will be hired by your current competitors or will join start-up enterprises aimed at becoming your competitors. All in all, a lot of related innovation and copying will be encouraged.

If your organization is large enough and can afford it, you can also consider establishing new departments of universities for the purposes of providing technical training. For the very biggest industry leaders, it's possible to create new universities, as General Motors did with its General Motors Institute (now known as Kettering University), and to provide extensive co-op education with your organization to learn applied skills.

Such programs offer another advantage for stimulating innovation: rapidly expanding the number of people with the knowledge, skills, and experience to innovate. As a result, the size of your innovation activities can be more substantially increased without hurting the quality of what you are doing.

What's the key lesson? *An industry-leading organization that sincerely wants to accelerate useful innovation can be helped by making it easier for students to master the tasks involved ... thus setting the bar higher for what the industry-leading organization will need to seek to accomplish for itself in innovation.*

Your Lesson Forty-Three Assignments

1. How could you and your stakeholders benefit because you sponsor university-research programs that make it easier for students to work for your organization, its competitors, and start-ups, increasing innovation and copying of what your organization does?

2. What would have to change about your innovation practices if competitors become more effective innovators and copiers due to your sponsoring university-research programs that expand the pool of qualified employees for innovating and copying?

3. How could you use making it easier for competitors to succeed by increasing the supply of those with knowledge, skills, and experience of innovating and copying due to sponsoring university-research programs as an advantage in stimulating your future innovations?

4. What could you do now to encourage making valuable innovations available sooner from your organization ...before considering the spur of current and future competitors more effectively developing new offerings?

5. How can you prepare in advance to enhance any gains from making it easier for your own organization and its competitors to have a much better and larger supply of innovative employees as a result of sponsoring university-research programs even more productive for your organization, your stakeholders, and everyone else in the industry?

Lesson Forty-Four

Sponsor Contests
To Reduce Costs
And Encourage
Competitors to Enter

Much food is in *the fallow* ground *of the poor,*
And for lack of justice there is waste.

— Proverbs 13:23 (NKJV)

How can you know when someone is truly poor? One strong indication is if someone must rely on his or her own agriculture, no matter how inefficient or ineffective, in order to eat. Proverbs 13:23 (NKJV) takes us back to when almost everyone lived in such circumstances. Naturally, if such a person could not farm all of the available ground, some of the opportunity to produce more food was lost. In addition, where justice does not reign, people have to make mighty efforts to gain what is rightfully theirs ... or not receive such substance at all. Any efforts by poor farmers that go into securing justice must come at the expense of activities that directly supply food and other necessities.

Clearly, there's needed some way for such poor people to become more productive that succeeds solely due to the efforts of others. In Biblical Israel, rich farmers were told to leave some of their crops to be gleaned by the poor. Our modern equivalent of this practice is the global contest designed to make breakthroughs for providing more benefits for all that engages those who can contribute and have the time and resources to do so.

The Ultimate Competitive Advantage, Business Basics, and *Excellent Solutions* discuss various ways that public contests can provide useful ideas and methods for 2,000 percent (20 times more with the same or less time, effort, and resources) and even greater improvements. These books recommend daily publishing of the best solution received so far and allowing anyone to improve upon that solution as a separate contest entry. This approach works well because many people can add or improve one element that greatly enhances a solution, while few can conceive of a totally new, superior approach on their own. In one online contest, the best solution using this method was more than 30 times more effective than in contests where entrants could not partially copy one another.

Here's a new wrinkle those books don't mention: Encourage competitors to fully participate in such a contest. In this way, you can greatly increase the stream of new ideas presented that they, too, can apply to their own businesses while giving them the opportunity to earn recognition for providing innovations that you can use. Naturally, the result in such a circumstance will be to encourage more innovation, and value will be enhanced for all stakeholders in the industry.

In this lesson and the next five, I describe public contests designed to enhance various aspects of innovation and copying. I address here the first such contest: ways to greatly reduce costs while providing at least the same kinds of and levels of benefits for stakeholders. If someone can reduce costs further while adding more benefits, those entries should also be encouraged as part of such a contest.

I believe that competitors will find it hard to resist such contests for the following six reasons:

1. Competitors probably have higher costs than you do now, and learning from your contest will seem like a necessary step for staying competitive in cost reductions.
2. It will be hard to resist gaining such insights for the mere cost (probably just some minimal time and effort) of registering as a competitor.
3. After competitors realize that individual solutions are greatly enhanced by gaining improvement ideas from others, competitors will appreciate that an important benefit can be obtained by sharing their own cost-reduction solutions.
4. If competitors do not propose cost innovations after entering the contest, there's a potential for their customers to wonder why they aren't working on finding ways to improve offerings and to potentially lower prices and customer costs.
5. Because competitors are weaker than your organization in at least some ways related to innovation, trying to compete by having their own contests would be hard to do well. Fewer people would be interested. The amount competitors could afford to pay in prizes would be smaller. If they tried and failed, their competitive stature would be further undermined with current and potential customers.
6. If the contest is defined in such a way that solutions are likely to apply to competitors, as well as to your own organization, competitors would be highly foolish not to participate. Investors and lenders might otherwise ask pointed questions.

To make this approach successful, such a contest has to be conducted a little differently from a proprietary contest. Let me explain what some of the adjustments might include. In doing so, realize that your competitors' reactions will probably be at least somewhat different from what I envision. So the most important point is that you encourage them to take a close look at your contest and to have sufficient time before the contest begins to make a well-considered decision about whether to participate. As a result, I suggest that you consider engaging in these five steps:

1. Post the proposed rules seeking comments for at least a 90-day period before the rules are finalized. Encourage people to suggest ways that the rules could be improved. The idea, of course, is to encourage competitors to indirectly float any reservations they have through suggestions made by third parties who are friendly with them. Change the rules to bring more competitors into the contest with fuller participation.

2. Avoid giving competitors an excuse for not participating due to their legal counsels not approving or there being some element of illegality involved. Gain official government review and advance approval, if necessary, so that no one will have a justified complaint if competitors participate. It may be that you'll need to ask a well-regarded independent third party to actually conduct the contest so that there won't be any hint of illegal collaboration among competitors. Seek good legal advice. Openly invite those with such concerns to express those issues during the comment period concerning the rules.

3. Be sure that everyone who participates can protect proprietary knowledge and intellectual property. If not, competitors may be afraid to participate for fear of unintentionally granting rights that would jeopardize their futures. Hire an intellectual-property attorney in your country to review the plans before proposing the initial set of rules for comment.

4. Avoid giving the impression that casual entrants are not welcome. Also be sure that customers, end users, suppliers, and other stakeholders realize that you welcome them being involved.

5. Ensure that the process of selecting and promoting solutions is seen as objective and aboveboard. Otherwise, such a contest could seem at first like a way to provide illegal gifts to people

your organization wants to favor for reasons unrelated to the contest itself.

If you decide you want to sponsor such a contest, please let me know by e-mail at donmitchell@fastforward400.com/. I'll be glad to assist you. Advising you will be a great way for me to learn, as well.

What's the key lesson? *An industry-leading organization that sincerely wants to accelerate its useful innovations can be helped by sponsoring contests that competitors can enter to find cost-reduction solutions that provide at least the current set and level of benefits to all stakeholders.*

Your Lesson Forty-Four Assignments

1. How could you and your stakeholders benefit because you seek to sponsor contests that competitors can enter to find cost-reduction solutions that provide at least the current set and level of benefits to all stakeholders?

2. If you seek to sponsor contests that competitors can enter to find cost-reduction solutions that provide at least the current set and level of benefits to all stakeholders, what would have to change about your innovation priorities, budgets, processes, and practices to encourage such a circumstance?

3. How could you use sponsoring contests that competitors can enter to find cost-reduction solutions that provide at least the current set and level of benefits to all stakeholders as an advantage in stimulating your future innovations?

4. What else could you do now to encourage making valuable innovations available much sooner from your organization ... beyond sponsoring contests that competitors can enter to find

cost-reduction solutions that provide at least the current set and level of benefits to all stakeholders?

5. How can you prepare in advance to make any gains from sponsoring contests that competitors can enter to find cost-reduction solutions that provide at least the current set and level of benefits to all stakeholders even more productive for your organization, your stakeholders, and the industry?

Lesson Forty-Five

Sponsor Contests to Inexpensively Combine Improvements for The First Time

*Let nothing be done through
selfish ambition or conceit, but
in lowliness of mind let each
esteem others better than himself.
Let each of you look out not only
for his own interests, but also
for the interests of others.*

— Philippians 2:3-4 (NKJV)

Philippians 2:3-4 (NKJV) reminds us that in applying Christ's charge to love others as He loves us that we need to look out for others, as well as for ourselves. What better way might we do that than by engaging more people in making worthy innovations that will expand His Kingdom? For this reason, the preceding lesson, this one, and the four that follow describe a series of public contests designed to encourage various helpful ways of innovating and copying. In this lesson, I address what I believe the second such contest should be:

ways to combine improvements for the first time at no higher cost for anyone. If someone can reduce costs further while adding more benefits, those entries should be encouraged as part of such a contest, as well.

Let me explain what I mean by combining improvements for the first time at no higher cost. I see such improvements as always increasing benefits received that customers and end users care about. Here's an example. Let's assume that you are a provider of professional services for improving your clients' effectiveness. You now offer two services: Training companies in how to apply Activity-Based Costing and Kaizen (the Japanese method of continuous improvement). These extensive, separate courses require many sessions that are expensive to provide, to take, and to apply.

A new solution would be to provide a combined course covering both topics in the same amount of time as the shorter of the present two courses at a price and cost no higher than the less expensive of the two. Thus, if the first course lasts eight days, costs $500 to provide, and your price is $1,000 and the second course lasts ten days, costs $700 to provide, and your price is $1,400, the newly combined course would last no longer than eight days, cost no more than $500 to provide, and would be priced at no more than $1,000. The combined course would have to be at least as effective for learning and application as the separate courses.

How might such a combination be accomplished? The Kaizen course could become the core of the new classes and Activity-Based Costing would be taught by documenting the primary Kaizen examples. You would eliminate the least effective aspects of the two separate courses, make the new course more interactive, supply more visual materials to concentrate the learning, test the students during the course, and make frequent adjustments to accelerate and improve learning. Other methods would probably also contribute value, such as tying what is learned more closely to the students' tasks at work.

I believe that competitors will find it hard to resist participating in such a contest about creating ways to combine improvements for the first time at no higher cost for anyone for the six reasons described in Lesson Forty-Four. As before, you should encourage their involvement. To make this approach successful, such a contest has to be conducted at first a little differently from a purely proprietary contest. The necessary adjustments are also listed in Lesson Forty-Four.

If you decide you want to sponsor such a contest, please let me know. I'll be glad to assist you. It will be a great way for me to learn, as well.

I believe that such contests will yield more innovative results than Lesson Forty-Four's cost-reduction contest will. That's because you could conduct many versions of the contest described in this lesson, with each one focused on combining benefit elements that had previously not been brought together.

As you could no doubt tell from my example, such contests are also likely to turn up important cost reductions that could potentially be applied in the absence of combining benefits. The advantages from these contests will become more significant when they occur after cost-reduction contests have already been conducted. In addition, some customers and end users won't benefit from combining certain kinds of benefits. Consequently, stand-alone offerings with fewer benefits will continue to be valuable in at least some cases, and these offerings should be made more cost efficient.

What's the key lesson? *An industry-leading organization that sincerely wants to accelerate its useful innovations can be helped by sponsoring contests that competitors can enter to find ways to combine benefit improvements for the first time at no higher price and cost.*

Your Lesson Forty-Five Assignments

1. How could you and your stakeholders benefit because you seek to sponsor contests that competitors can enter to find solutions that combine benefit improvements for the first time at no higher price and cost for your organization or any stakeholder?

2. If you seek to sponsor contests that competitors can enter to find ways to combine benefit improvements for the first time at no higher price and cost, what would have to change about your innovation priorities, budgets, processes, and practices to encourage such a circumstance?

3. How could you use sponsoring contests that competitors can enter to find ways to combine benefit improvements for the first time at no higher price and cost as an advantage in stimulating your future innovations?

4. What else could you do now to encourage making valuable innovations available much sooner from your organization ... beyond sponsoring contests that competitors can enter to find ways to combine benefit improvements for the first time at no higher price and cost?

5. How can you prepare in advance to make any gains in increasing competitors' innovations and copying from sponsoring contests that competitors can enter to find ways to combine benefit improvements for the first time at no higher price and cost even more productive for your organization, your stakeholders, and the industry?

Lesson Forty-Six

Sponsor Contests
To Improve Design
At Lower Cost

Thus he made the ten carts.
All of them were of the same mold,
one measure, and one shape.

— 1 Kings 7:37 (NKJV)

1 Kings (NKJV) contains many specific instructions for the construction of King Solomon's Temple. Clearly, some images and shapes are more pleasing to God than are others. Since we are made in God's image then we, too, should have preferences that He intended for certain images and shapes. Whether our offerings are products, services, or some combination of the two, it is well worth providing something that is more pleasing to use and to see. While sometimes design provides functional advantages, other times the benefits may be purely aesthetic. Don't neglect one for the other. Instead, provide more of each.

In this lesson, I address what I believe the third in the series of public contests should be: improved design at lower cost. If someone can also add new benefits at the same time, that option should definitely be encouraged in the contest.

Let me explain what I mean by an improved design at lower cost. If you think of physical products, naturally they have a shape, a number of components or elements that also have shapes and are exposed or hidden, various colors placed in different locations, and other appearance characteristics affected by the types of finish. Look at a variety of cellular telephones, smartphones, tablets, and laptops to get a sense of how important such design characteristics can be.

When it comes to larger items, such as furniture, vehicles, and homes, design becomes more important. But design can also be critical for something quite small, such as a knife that also contains many tools. The same is true for watches. An elegant design often attracts us more than the actual utility of various other tools, mechanisms, and gadgets.

Keep in mind that many intangible products also have design features, such as electronic offerings. When you look at electronic, intangible products, design is mostly what you see until you begin examining a specific user feature, such as a word in a text file or a processing routine in a software package.

Even services that you don't see happening directly, such as a securities trade, show design elements on the display screens and the confirmation reports that you receive.

Design is all around us, and we judge a lot by appearance ... just as we tend to give more credit to handsome men and beautiful women ... and to well-dressed people who use styles and apparel combinations that we like. It's such second nature for us to respond to design that we often don't realize when we are doing it. Most people will equate the offering that has the design they most like with being the "best" offering.

Design isn't limited to just appearance. Design can also improve functionality. A physical offering with fewer components will usually be less expensive to make and to provide, and such an offering will probably have fewer failures while in use. That's just because there are fewer steps for producing the offering, as well as fewer things that can go wrong.

However, simpler isn't always better. Occasionally, adding a component may actually reduce costs for customers and manufacturers. I saw such an example when our home hot-water heater failed.

Since we bought our last hot-water heater, a new design was developed providing the option to insert an extra piece of metal into the tank that draws away some of the corrosive elements in the water so that they are less attracted to the glass lining that keeps the hot-water heater free of leaks. By adding this one component, the life of a tank is approximately doubled, reducing the annual cost of purchasing and installing a tank by almost 50 percent. Since these hot-water heaters come with warranties, the warranty cost is going to be lower with the tanks that insert the extra component. That's clearly a lower-cost design, even though the original purchase price is increased by about 13 percent.

Likewise, an intangible offering that is simpler to provide and simpler to use will be less costly and cause fewer irritations. In the United States, insurance policies for about any purpose are dozens of pages long and produced in very small type. Unless you spend many hours studying them, it's hard to know what your coverage is. If you ask an agent or someone at the insurance company, you will usually be given incorrect information. If you are harmed in the process, the insurance company and agent will avoid taking any blame. Consequently, I'm sure that some people would be attracted to insurance policies that are easy to understand and make receiving payments easier after an incident occurs.

Providing an offering also has business-model elements that can make an offering more appealing or can reduce costs. Have you ever been asked to follow an online process that took you through what seemed to be an unending number of screens with fairly ambiguous directions about where to go next and that presented great difficulties for going back if you had made a mistake? Surely, some of the process steps could have been eliminated ... thus, providing a much more pleasing customer or end-user experience.

As I mention in Lesson Forty-Four, I believe that competitors will find it hard to resist participating in a contest to improve design at lower cost for the six reasons described there. As before, you should encourage competitors' involvement. To make this approach successful, such a contest has to be conducted at first a little differently from a purely proprietary contest. The necessary adjustments are also listed in Lesson Forty-Four.

If you decide you want to sponsor such a contest, please let me know. I'll be glad to assist you. It will be a great way for me to learn, as well.

I believe that such contests will yield highly innovative results because you will be looking for designs that enhance benefits and lower costs for the breakthrough solutions developed by your prior contests that sought lower cost alternatives and combining previously uncombined benefits less expensively.

What's the key lesson? *An industry-leading organization that sincerely wants to accelerate its useful innovations can be helped by sponsoring contests that competitors can enter to improve design at lower cost.*

Your Lesson Forty-Six Assignments

1. How could you and your stakeholders benefit because you seek to sponsor contests that competitors can enter to improve designs at lower cost?

2. If you seek to sponsor contests that competitors can enter to improve designs at lower cost, what would have to change about your innovation priorities, budgets, processes, and practices to encourage such a circumstance?

3. How could you use sponsoring contests that competitors can enter to improve designs at lower cost as an advantage in stimulating your future innovations?

4. What else could you do now to encourage making valuable innovations available much sooner from your organization ... beyond sponsoring contests that competitors can enter to improve designs at lower cost?

5. How can you prepare in advance to make any gains in increasing competitors' copying from sponsoring contests that competitors can enter to improve designs at lower cost even more productive for your organization, your stakeholders, and the industry?

Lesson Forty-Seven

Sponsor Contests To Improve Convenience At Lower Cost With Less Waste

"And not many days after,
the younger son gathered all together,
journeyed to a far country,
and there wasted his possessions
with prodigal living."

— Luke 15:13 (NKJV)

God uses everything. When Jesus multiplied the loaves to feed first 5,000 men and later 4,000 men (plus untold numbers of women and children), He directed the disciples to pick up the leftover pieces. Unlike God, we tend to be pleasure seeking and wasteful. Jesus' parable of the Prodigal Son (told in Luke 15, NKJV) captures that part of our essence. From the contrast, we can surely appreciate the possibility that God will approve of reasonable things being done to reduce costs and waste in ways that will appeal to His people who are seeking convenience. This lesson focuses on having a fourth public contest to improve offering convenience at lower cost and with less waste. If someone can add new benefits at the same time, that option should definitely be encouraged in the contest.

Let me explain what I mean by an offering with improved convenience at lower cost and with less waste. Here's a definition of *convenience* from www.dictionary.com: "anything that saves or simplifies work, adds to one's ease or comfort, etc., as an appliance, utensil, or the like."

Convenience is important because most people feel they have too little time to do what they want to accomplish. If you look at most product and service categories, one of the important characteristics of the market leader is often providing more convenience that saves time, effort, and stress on customers and end users.

Let's begin with convenience as it applies to products. As you have no doubt experienced, many products are not very convenient. Consider the new water heater I wrote about in the preceding lesson. The directions call for draining several quarts of water once a week for the next ten years! That's over 520 trips to the water heater.

I don't know where your water heater is located, but ours is in the darkest, most remote part of our cellar. You practically need a guide to get there. The nearest appropriate drain for dumping the water is more than fifty feet away and up a narrow flight of steps to the next level. So you have to remove the water and then carry it up to drain it. Water is heavy and can be messy if you spill it.

What are the chances that someone will perform this maintenance? Well, not very high in our house. So far, it hasn't happened once.

The directions also explain that if you replace the rod designed to keep the glass lining from wearing out when it's at a certain point of erosion, you will be able to keep the water heater going indefinitely. But as I read the instructions, I had no idea what they were talking about concerning when to replace the rod. I also couldn't figure out how I was supposed to inspect the rod, even if I could determine that it was time to replace it.

Now, this is a pretty expensive piece of equipment. You would think that either the methods for keeping it going could be made simpler ... or at least the directions could be understandable by someone other than a plumber. For instance, the hot water could simply be pulled through the house from the bottom, rather than from the top, of the tank, and many fewer harmful sediments would build up to erode the glass lining at the bottom. Or the glass lining at the bottom could have many extra layers to help resist sediment reaching and breaching the metal in the tank.

You probably have your own examples of such products that could be much improved by providing more convenience.

Waste is expensive, and more and more people have little patience for unnecessary waste. Reduce waste in helpful ways, and many people will be agreeable to paying a premium. That's clearly the case with the hybrid vehicles that use less gasoline for fuel. Such vehicles cost so much more than conventional ones that gasoline prices would have to rise to much higher levels before anyone could expect to get a return on such an investment. But the desires to reduce petroleum use and to pollute less are strong among some people, and such vehicles sell quite well. Surely, the convenience of not making as many stops at gas stations is also part of the appeal of these vehicles.

The point about reducing waste can also be exemplified by the water heater. When one of these tanks fails, it's because the bottom rusts out. So you have some steel that can be salvaged, along with lots of rusty water all over the area where the hot-water heater is. The plumber told me that in most homes in our area water heaters last about six years. That relatively short life means that many water heaters are being scrapped at any point in time, while water heaters with better designs and maintenance could last indefinitely. Certainly, that's a lot of waste that can be reduced. The cost savings for consumers are potentially huge over a lifetime.

Here's another example of waste. A former student told me about a product his company made. For decades, more than 98 percent of the ingredients were dumped into the ocean after the production process was completed. The student was able to find ways to upgrade almost all of those ingredients into other products that he sold at a profit, an innovation that soon led him into the ranks of top management for a very large organization.

As you must have experienced, services can be even bigger sources of inconvenience and waste. Let me share a recent example. In the United States, most people have private health insurance, mostly paid for by their employers as a tax-free benefit. Sounds good, doesn't it? Well, try to get some medicine through such an insurer, and you may soon be tearing out your hair.

A friend of mine has a prescription that she's been taking for many years. When her employer changed insurers, the new insurance company refused to honor the prescription ... insisting that she use a less costly medicine. My friend had to go through several medicines before she found one that seemed to work all right.

To get any of the medicine, it had to be ordered through the insurance company. Then my friend got a new prescription from her physician for the insurance-approved medicine. The prescription was for 27 doses. She received only 9 doses in the mail and a bill for her portion of the prescription for 27 doses. Sorting this out took over an hour on the telephone, and she had conversations with more than six people to accomplish it. She had to waste all this time, or be overcharged and not receive enough medicine. The entire burden was on her. There was no burden on the insurance company to provide a benefit. By eliminating the errors involved in orders, insurance costs could be lower, and much time wasting would be eliminated.

As I mention in Lesson Forty-Four, I believe (and hope) that competitors will find it hard to resist participating in a contest to improve convenience at lower cost with less waste for the six reasons described there. As before, you should encourage their involvement. To make this approach successful, such a contest has to be conducted at first a little differently from a purely proprietary contest. The necessary adjustments are also listed in Lesson Forty-Four.

If you decide you want to sponsor such a contest, please let me know. I'll be glad to assist you. It will be a great way for me to learn, as well.

I believe that such contests will yield highly innovative results because you will be looking for convenience-improving and waste-reducing innovations that enhance and lower costs for the break-through solutions resulting from your prior contests for lowering costs, combining previously uncombined benefits, and providing better designs at lower cost.

What's the key lesson? *An industry-leading organization that sincerely wants to accelerate its useful innovations can be helped by sponsoring contests that competitors can enter to find ways to improve convenience and reduce waste at lower cost.*

Your Lesson Forty-Seven Assignments

1. How could you and your stakeholders benefit because you seek to sponsor contests that competitors can enter to improve convenience and reduce waste at lower cost?

2. If you seek to sponsor contests that competitors can enter to improve convenience and reduce waste at lower cost, what would have to change about your innovation priorities, budgets, processes, and practices to encourage such a circumstance?

3. How could you use sponsoring contests that competitors can enter to improve convenience and reduce waste at lower cost as an advantage in stimulating your future innovations?

4. What else could you do now to encourage making valuable innovations available much sooner from your organization ... beyond sponsoring contests that competitors can enter to improve convenience and reduce waste at lower cost?

5. How can you prepare in advance to make any gains in increasing competitors' innovation and copying from sponsoring contests that competitors can enter to improve convenience and reduce waste at lower cost even more productive for your organization, your stakeholders, and the industry?

Lesson Forty-Eight

Sponsor Contests For Providing Highly Unique, Custom Offerings At Lower Cost

And he prepared the inner sanctuary inside the temple,
to set the ark of the covenant of the LORD there.
The inner sanctuary was twenty cubits long,
twenty cubits wide, and twenty cubits high.
He overlaid it with pure gold,
and overlaid the altar of cedar.
So Solomon overlaid the inside
of the temple with pure gold.
He stretched gold chains across the front
of the inner sanctuary, and overlaid it with gold.
The whole temple he overlaid with gold,
until he had finished all the temple;
also he overlaid with gold the entire altar
that was by the inner sanctuary.

— 1 Kings 6:19-22 (NKJV)

Was there ever a more important building project than Solomon's Temple? God cared about how His Temple would look, providing many specific directions for Solomon and the builders to follow. In these verses from 1 Kings 6 (NKJV), we see some of the custom work required to create the Holy of Holies, where the Ark of the Covenant would rest. While God can always supply what's needed to create something that needs to be customized just so, surely He would like the work done better, faster, and less expensively so that time, money, and effort would remain for use in other ways to expand His Kingdom.

This lesson addresses what I believe the fifth such public contest should be: creating a process for making highly unique, custom products and related services at lower cost. If someone can add other benefits at the same time, that option should definitely be encouraged in the contest.

Let me start by explaining what I mean by highly unique custom products and related services at lower cost. I have two examples in mind.

The first product is custom-fitted clothing in the same styles as are shown on fashion-show runways, provided at the price and cost of ready-to-wear clothing. Since these styles would be quite fresh, those who wore them first would be unlikely to find a custom-fit look-alike while attending a public event. Naturally, there would soon be ready-to-wear rip-offs available, but those clothes would poorly hang on their wearers rather than have that great custom-fit look.

The second product that intrigues me is custom granola, prepared to reflect the exact taste preferences of the eater. While many companies offer varieties of unique granolas, the products are usually quite expensive and there's no opportunity to make custom versions. Naturally, you can mix and make your own, but a great food company should be able to concoct something that suits your fancy better than what you produce for yourself ... at the cost of standard branded granolas (unless you want very expensive ingredients).

Next, let me explain what I mean by related services for such custom products. Focusing first on custom designer clothing at ready-to-wear prices, one such service might involve simulated versions of the custom designer clothes that are being considered arrayed on that person's image along with items already owned by this person. Doing so would enable a purchaser to see how well she or he would look in ensembles involving some existing clothing and accessories along with the new clothing. In addition to presenting the "look" visually, such software might also make suggestions for other colors, items, and combinations of what the potential purchaser already owns for a more attractive wardrobe at less total expense.

In terms of the custom-made granola, many people like variety. A related service might be to help people plan complementary meals that would provide more helpful nutrients for someone eating a particular type of granola at the time.

Obviously, such products and related services would be in great demand if they were easy to acquire and inexpensive. Making such improvements provides the basis for a public contest.

Undoubtedly, special kinds of equipment will need to be developed. Low-cost ways of ordering and funneling supplies will be needed. Manufacturing will probably need to be dispersed so it can be done relatively near to where the end users are. Otherwise, waits for the custom products might negate many of the desired benefits, especially when it comes to designer clothes at ready-to-wear prices. Someone may be ordering a special dress just for an occasion that came up at the last minute.

In most industries, very little work will have been done in advance on such concepts. Why? Most organizations favor methods of mass provision, whether for products or services. There may be some customization opportunities, such as with personal computers made by Dell, but typically the idea is to only do so when profits will be higher.

In these cases, the focus will be on adding more value for the amounts of money that some people already pay for items of lesser desirability. In the process of shifting to provision of such custom items at standard prices, a whole industry can be transformed and its size greatly increased. It sounds like fun, doesn't it?

As I mention in Lesson Forty-Four, I believe that competitors will find it hard to resist participating in a contest for creating a process for making highly unique, custom products and related services at lower cost for the six reasons described there. As before, you should encourage competitors' involvement. To make this approach successful, such a contest has to be conducted at first a little differently from a purely proprietary contest. The necessary adjustments are also listed in Lesson Forty-Four.

If you decide you want to sponsor such a contest, please let me know. I'll be glad to assist you. It will be a great way for me to learn, as well.

I believe that such contests will yield highly innovative results because you will be looking for something that everyone will perceive as having the potential for making breakthroughs: customizing offerings at everyday prices.

What's the key lesson? *An industry-leading organization that sincerely wants to accelerate its useful innovations can be helped by sponsoring contests that competitors can enter to find ways to customize offerings and related services at lower costs so that prices can be the same as for standard items that everyone thinks are affordable.*

Your Lesson Forty-Eight Assignments

1. How could you and your stakeholders benefit because you seek to sponsor contests that competitors can enter to customize offerings and related services at low cost?

2. If you seek to sponsor contests that competitors can enter to customize offerings and related services at low cost, what would

have to change about your innovation priorities, budgets, processes, and practices to encourage such a circumstance?

3. How could you use sponsoring contests that competitors can enter to customize offerings and related services at low cost as an advantage in stimulating your future innovations?

4. What else could you do now to encourage making valuable innovations available much sooner from your organization ... beyond sponsoring contests that competitors can enter to customize offerings and related services at low cost?

5. How can you prepare in advance to make any gains in increasing competitors' innovation and copying from sponsoring contests that competitors can enter to customize offerings and related services at low cost even more productive for your organization, your stakeholders, and the industry?

Lesson Forty-Nine

Sponsor Contests to Create Offerings That Are Quickly Profitable for Customers and End Users

"For what will it profit a man
if he gains the whole world,
and loses his own soul?"

— Mark 8:36 (NKJV)

Jesus' words in Mark 8:36 (NKJV) are a good reminder that spiritual gains should be sought ahead of Earthly profits. With that reminder in front of us, we should be sure that our contests advance His Kingdom as their primary focus. In doing so, however, adding some Earthly benefits to spiritual gains is certainly something to consider, just as long as the benefits don't come at the expense of the spiritual gains.

In this lesson, I propose the sixth and final type of contest in the series: creating offerings that quickly provide spiritual and economic benefits for customers and end users.

Let me start by explaining what I mean by offerings that are rapidly profitable for customers and end users. Let me explain by use of an example. Imagine that you sell, lease, or rent business vans. As part of such offerings, you also provide each purchaser, lessee, or renter with a guide to earning money in 1,001 different ways by using a business van and a membership to a Web site that has hundreds of leads from nearby people who want services that require a business van. Done properly, the new possessor of the van should be able to use the guide and Web-site membership to obtain enough work to more than pay for the van during the same time period and to earn an above-average income for whatever time is involved in using the van for business purposes. If the person doing this work is encouraged to share the Gospel and to show God's love, spiritual riches will be added for one and all.

The reason this concept is important is that it enables anyone who can meet credit requirements to obtain access to resources that make it possible to earn an above-average income. In the van example, someone who could only afford to rent the van for a few hours would thus be able to obtain enough work to eventually rent a van for a few days, later lease one for months at a time, and potentially to eventually purchase one.

By demonstrating an ability to earn money with the van, it would also be possible to qualify renters, lessees, and purchasers for better credit terms so that even smaller advance payments or credit card holds would be required.

The result of achieving such a purpose will be to vastly increase consumption by drawing customers away from other purchases and ways of earning money.

Naturally, this concept will be harder to apply to many human basics such as food, but the challenge may bring out ways to add value that no one has previously considered. For instance, someone who does piecework might be willing to pay for nutritional supplements that make her or him feel more peaceful and energetic so that the work can be finished faster or more accurately, thus increasing income.

While many offerings are sold, in part, on the premise that the purchaser will earn a profit from acquiring them, in practice the profit potential may be iffy ... depending on the overall market for products and services, the effectiveness of the person acquiring the offering, and temporary conditions. As a result, many people acquire offerings that don't pay off for them. A typical example would be taking a business course, but never applying anything that is learned to a business. There's no way to earn a profit or a spiritual advantage from such a lack of using an offering. The results of a contest for creating offerings that are quickly profitable for customers and end users should eliminate such misfires and wasted time and resources.

As I mention in Lesson Forty-Four, I believe that competitors will find it hard to resist participating in a contest for creating offerings that are quickly profitable for customers and end users for the six reasons described there. As before, you should encourage competitors' involvement. To make this approach successful, such a contest has to be conducted at first a little differently from a purely proprietary contest. The necessary adjustments are also listed in Lesson Forty-Four.

If you decide you want to sponsor a contest for creating offerings that are quickly profitable for customers and end users, please let me know. I'll be glad to assist you. It will be a great way for me to learn, as well.

I believe that such contests will yield highly innovative results because you will be looking for something that everyone will perceive as having the potential for making breakthroughs: turning offerings into fast sources of spiritual benefits and economic value.

What's the key lesson? *An industry-leading organization that sincerely wants to accelerate its useful innovations can be helped by sponsor-*

ing contests that competitors can enter to find ways to make offerings *quickly and greatly useful to customers and end users in terms of spiritual and economic benefits.*

Your Lesson Forty-Nine Assignments

1. How could you and your stakeholders benefit because you sponsor contests that competitors can enter to create offerings that quickly provide customers and end users with spiritual and economic benefits?

2. If you seek to sponsor contests that competitors can enter to create offerings that quickly deliver spiritual and economic benefits, what would have to change about your innovation priorities, budgets, processes, and practices to encourage achieving such a circumstance?

3. How could you use sponsoring contests that competitors can enter to create offerings that quickly provide spiritual and economic benefits as an advantage in stimulating your organization's future innovations?

4. What else could you do now to encourage making valuable innovations available much sooner from your organization ... beyond sponsoring contests that competitors can enter to create offerings that quickly deliver spiritual and economic benefits to customers and end users?

5. How can you prepare in advance to make more valuable for your company, its stakeholders, and the industry any gains in increasing competitors' innovation and copying from sponsoring contests that competitors can enter to create offerings that quickly provide customers and end users with spiritual and economic benefits?

Lesson Fifty

Expand Demand Far Beyond Industry Capacity

"Bring all the tithes into the storehouse,
That there may be food in My house,
And try Me now in this,"
Says the LORD of hosts,
"If I will not open for you
the windows of heaven
And pour out for you such *blessing*
That there will *not* be
room *enough* to receive it."*

— Malachi 3:10 (NKJV)

In Malachi 3:10 (NKJV), God reminds His people to bring the first 10 percent of their increase to the Temple. In today's world, many pastors interpret this passage as meaning that a similar amount of one's income should be provided to the local church. For our purposes, note that God talks about providing blessing that exceeds the room an individual has to receive it. We should always learn to be more generous from God's example. Someone who receives so much from God will often choose to make additional offerings for His purposes, including more gifts to the local church, as well as providing for others to advance God's Kingdom.

As applied to a business, the lesson is to be so generous in stimulating demand for the industry's offerings that all of our competitors will prosper. Obviously, if offerings are so much sought after, the benefits for stakeholders, especially customers and end users, will also be enormous.

You probably have some questions about what will happen if you do so. Let me pose and answer some of the questions that you may have.

Why will expanding demand far beyond industry capacity stimulate competitors' innovations and copying of what you do? Such conditions are favorable for unusually high profit margins and reduce the risk of loss for those who enter an industry. Because of the perceived profit potential, most new entrants will take the fastest route ... which means producing offerings very similar to what you provide using facilities that are very much like yours with a business model that's comparable. New entrants also tend to overestimate the future demand for offerings, which will often lock them into large-scale investments that cannot easily be changed. With such large investment in place, any time that their growth slows down such new entrants will be eagerly watching for your next innovation so that can copy it.

Why will attracting more innovating and copying competitors help your organization to be more innovative? First, a lot of the energy that might otherwise go into expanding your organization to accommodate all the potential demand in the industry can be directed into innovation rather than into multiplication of yesterday's and today's activities.

Second, having so many more hungry competitors with an eye focused on copying and improving what you do means that the advantages you gain from innovation will be sooner negated by such competitive activities. Your organization's innovators will want to be faster and more effective in innovating in order to keep a more comfortable degree of advantage over the alternative offerings on the market.

Third, in such an environment many of your colleagues will receive tempting employment offers from companies that are entering the industry. By some realizing that by leaving they can make a lot more money and enjoy a better career, the people who remain will be more focused on the joy of innovation as their reason for being with your organization. With those who are less committed to innovation winnowed out, the remaining people will be able to operate with fewer restraints on what they want to do. Consequently, their rate of improvement should improve.

Fourth, realizing that almost everyone else in the industry may be more interested in copying and making a lot of money for doing it than in fundamental innovating, those stakeholders who would like to improve offerings will feel a stronger need to first bring their ideas and assistance to your organization. As a result, you'll have stronger support from your current and potential stakeholders.

Fifth, as your organization's reputation for innovation expands, those customers and end users who crave new and improved offerings will increase their attention on your organization, making those who work on innovation even more aware that their improved offerings will be well accepted by current customers and end users.

How can you accomplish expanding demand far beyond industry capacity? This subject was indirectly addressed by the first lessons in *Business Basics*. I refer you to those lessons for ideas. To those ideas, let me add some ways to be sure that industry capacity lags far behind demand. In sharing these suggestions, I do not mean for them to be encyclopedic, but rather illustrative, of what can be accomplished:

First, consider desirable ways to innovate for expanding the market that will have constrained capacity because of sourcing limitations. I read about an example recently that nicely illustrated this opportunity. An importer in the United States wanted to offer unique individual pieces of upholstered furniture. When considering Pakistan as a potential source, the importer noticed that many unique rugs are handmade there. The company decided to take outstanding rugs

313

made there and to cut them into pieces suitable for upholstering furniture. Because of tastes in the United States, only a small percentage of the designs were appropriate for the purpose. After determining what the right quality standard was for the fabric, the importer arranged to view images of the rugs meeting the standard so that it could have first pick of the best designs. By setting in place a supply chain that selected from tens of thousands of rugs, anyone who copied this product concept would be using designs or rug qualities that were inferior to the innovator's offerings. These one of a kind items often sold for $3,000 to $4,000 each at retail in the United States with a sourcing cost of less than $700 each.

Second, use scarcity as part of the appeal for faster market expansion. In past lessons in other 400 Year Project books, we have discussed that helping customers and end users to appreciate that a new offering is genuinely in limited supply will often cause an enormous increase in demand as people "stock up" on what won't be available again for some time. The furniture importer could have built its appeal by indicating that it would put 10,000 rugs on its Web site for customers to choose from that had been checked for quality of materials and appearance and then let customers know that when these rugs were gone there would be no more upholstered furniture offered that year. Any customers who wanted to furnish a room with such furniture that complemented each other piece would then order quickly while selection was at its best. Those who simply wanted a design they loved for one item of furniture would also be in a hurry to pick one out.

Third, engage customers you cannot serve immediately by providing some advantage that makes it worthwhile to wait for you to provide for them. In the upholstered furniture case, this advantage might be giving those who made a substantial deposit the right to pick ahead of everyone else the next time that such an item was made available. Then, publicize how many people are on the waiting list. Many potential customers will be impressed and seek to gain a similar advantage for themselves. The more people on the waiting list, the more competitors will copy. If they cannot compete with you by using Pakistani rugs, they may try to do the same thing with rugs from some other nation where the designs and quality aren't as good. Because you want to encourage copying, you should leave such less desirable supply sources in place for copiers.

Fourth, publicize information that will let everyone know that demand far exceeds supply. For instance, you might keep track of how many unique visitors come to your Web site compared to how many items you can provide. If you were the furniture importer, you might be able to report than hundreds of times more people visited than the 10,000 items that you could actually produce in the current year.

Fifth, if you find ways to innovate that will greatly expand supply, keep that information secret as long as possible. An obvious innovation for such an industry is to work with customers to create designs that they would like to have produced and arrange for those designs to be hand woven in conformance with the quality specifications you find to be appropriate. In this way, uniqueness is maintained while the ability to furnish more rooms in more compatible ways is increased. Naturally, if you contract for the capacity of the best custom weavers, you'll have just created another scarcity.

Sixth, create a series of innovations that will each have a scarce quality. For instance, at some point you could arrange for top designers to create limited editions of their unique designs. By contracting with the top designers in advance, competitors will have to go to less well-known and less appealing designers. As you do, keep removing limitations on industry supply while still keeping demand well above supply.

I'm sure you get the idea. I will look forward to hearing about the innovative new businesses you develop that take advantage of this approach to encouraging copying.

What's the key lesson? *An industry-leading organization that sincerely wants to accelerate its useful innovations can be helped by expanding demand far beyond industry capacity while retaining competitive advantages for itself.*

Your Lesson Fifty Assignments

1. How could you and your stakeholders benefit because you stimulate demand far beyond industry capacity while retaining competitive advantages for your organization?

2. If you stimulate demand far beyond industry capacity while retaining competitive advantages for your organization, what would have to change about your innovation priorities, budgets, processes, and practices to encourage such a circumstance?

3. How could you use stimulating demand far beyond industry capacity while retaining competitive advantages for your organization as a help in increasing your future innovations?

4. What else could you do now to encourage making valuable innovations available much sooner from your organization ... beyond stimulating demand far beyond industry capacity while retaining competitive advantages for your organization?

5. How can you prepare in advance to make any gains in increasing competitors' innovation and copying by stimulating demand far beyond industry capacity while retaining competitive advantages for your organization even more productive for your organization, your stakeholders, and the industry?

Appendix

Donald Mitchell's Testimony

He will lift you up.

Humble yourselves
in the sight of the Lord,
and He will lift you up.

— James 4:10 (NKJV)

Let me share with you how I became a Christian so you'll know where I'm coming from with regard to encouraging you to become a Christian and to be fruitful in Godly contributions for creating and implementing breakthrough solutions.

There has been a long commitment to the Lord in our family. For example, I remember my great-grandmother, Edith Foster, reading the Bible every day. As a youngster, my mother regularly took me to Sunday school. It was my least favorite activity; sleeping was much preferred. I did enjoy listening to sermons, but it was frowned on to take youngsters to the adult services where the sermons were given.

If I pretended to be asleep, mom would sometimes let me stay home on Sundays. I was pretty good at pretending, and I soon was the biggest backslider in my Sunday school grade. Fortunately, it was an evangelical church so my classmates were always cooking up schemes to get me to attend again. Because of my high opinion of myself, I would always return if invited to play my clarinet for the congregation.

By the time I turned thirteen, I was pretty full of myself. There wasn't much room for God in there alongside my exaggerated opinion of myself.

One day at home while my family was away for a drive, I felt really sick. By the time they returned, I was delirious. Within an hour, I was in the hospital where I would stay for two weeks as I barely survived a bad case of double pneumonia.

My physician, Dr. Helmsley, was an observant Christian and worried about my soul because my life was in jeopardy. He talked to me about our Heavenly Father, Jesus, and the Holy Spirit twice a day when he stopped by to check on me. These conversations were when I first learned how to become a Christian through being born again. I also came to realize that I couldn't stop sinning on my own. I needed a Savior, Jesus Christ! After I recovered, he took my mom and me to a tent revival meeting.

Having recovered from the illness, I soon pushed God out of my life again. During the next year, I was, instead, very caught up in athletics. When I was in ninth grade, I desperately wanted to make a contribution to our junior high track team, which had a remote chance of winning the big meet. Our coach, Mr. Layman, told each of us exactly what had to be accomplished for the team to win. I was determined to do my part. I had to come in first!

But that wasn't likely to happen. Based on past performances, there were at least two people who could out leap me in the standing broad jump, my main event. To make such a jump, you stand on a slightly raised, forward-tilted board and spring outward as far as you can into a sand-filled pit. After two of the three jumping rounds, I knew it was hopeless. I was in sixth place and four of the competitors' jumps were longer than I had ever gone before. I also didn't like the board we were using.

Remembering that we should call on God when we need help, I thought of praying ... but what I wanted was so trivial in God's terms that I didn't think it was worthy of prayer. So I decided to make God an offer instead: "Dear God, help me win this event, and I'm yours forever." After all, if He came through, any doubts I had about God would be dispelled.

I stepped onto the broad-jump board and felt very calm. I did my routine and took off into the air. Instantly, I felt light as a feather cradled in a large, gentle hand that was lifting me. I was dropped softly at the far end of the pit. I had outleapt everyone and gone more than six inches past my best previous jump. I couldn't believe it. Then I remembered my promise to God, thanked Him, repented my sins, accepted Jesus as my Lord and Savior, and ran off to tell everyone on the team.

Even more remarkable, I was the only person on the team who performed up to the plan. Knowing what had to be done had probably given us performance anxiety, and people underperformed because they didn't believe they could do what the team needed. I also suspect that God wanted to make a point with me that I needed Him.

After a few days, I started to think that perhaps I'd just developed a new broad-jump technique and God didn't have a role at all. God soon dispelled that thought by making sure that my jumps for the rest of my life were much shorter than I had jumped when He lifted me up.

Since then, God has been speaking to me on a regular basis through the Holy Spirit. I have learned to pay attention and act promptly. When I pursue my own ideas, things don't go so well. When I follow His directions, things work out great. That's my secret to high performance, and I just wanted to share it with you so you could benefit, too. He knows the answers, even when you and I don't ... which is most of the time.

As a management consultant, the Holy Spirit has often filled me with knowledge about what the consequences of one set of actions would be compared to another for my clients. Naturally, I always recommended as the Holy Spirit directed me. Clients often told me that they were impressed by how certain I was of my conclusions and of how persuasive I could be in describing the advantages of whatever recommendations were made. Once again, the explanatory words came from the Holy Spirit, rather than from me.

Unfortunately, I wasn't comfortable in my younger days sharing my faith with clients, and I wrongly gave many people the impression that I was the author of the solutions rather than merely the transmitter. I wish I had been more faithful in this regard. I apologize to my clients for having missed so many great witnessing opportunities with them.

I didn't always listen as well as I should in making decisions that primarily affected me, but God would always do something to get my attention. Here's an example. I made an investment that I hoped would reduce my taxes in addition to making some money. I didn't have a good feeling from the Holy Spirit at the time, and I shouldn't have invested.

My tax return was later audited by the Internal Revenue Service concerning that investment. It turned out I was in the wrong for the deductions I had taken. Anticipating a big tax bill plus penalties and interest, you can imagine my astonishment when the revised tax return showed me owing no additional money to the government even though I had lost on the audit issues. I knew that result was a gift from God, and I was overwhelmed by His wisdom and power in protecting me. Praise God for His mercy!

I rededicated my life to Jesus in 1995, and I have enjoyed great peace since then. I have also done a lot better in being obedient to the Holy Spirit and to what the Bible tells us to do in all aspects of my life. Many blessings have been mine since then.

After being told by God to start The 400 Year Project (demonstrating how everyone in the world could make improvements twenty times faster and more effectively than normal with no additional resources) in 1995, I continued to receive His instructions. In

2005, for example, God told me to start explaining to people how to live their lives by gaining more joy from what they already have.

In the summer of 2006, I began to see how The 400 Year Project could be brought to a successful conclusion (as I reported in *Adventures of an Optimist*, Mitchell and Company Press, 2007). Realizing that perhaps I had devoted too much of my attention to this one challenge, I began to seek ways to rebalance my life. One of those rebalancing methods was to spend more time communing with God through prayer, Scriptural studies, attending church services and Bible classes, and listening more to the still, small voice within.

For several years I had been enjoying the devotionals sent to me daily over the Internet by evangelist Bill Keller. One of those devotionals speared me like an arrow that summer. The evangelist reminded his readers that our responsibility as believers is to share our faith with others through our example and sharing the Gospel message from the Bible. Not feeling well equipped to do more than try to be a good example, I began to pray about what else I should be doing.

The next day, my answer came: I was to launch a global contest to locate the most effective ways that souls were being saved and be sure that information was shared widely. This sharing would be a blessing for those who wished to fulfill the Great Commission to spread the Good News of Jesus as commanded in Matthew 28:18-20 (NKJV):

And Jesus came and spoke to them, saying, "All authority has been given to Me in heaven and on earth. Go therefore and make disciples of all the nations, baptizing them in the name of the Father and of the Son and of the Holy Spirit, teaching them to observe all things that I have commanded you; and lo, I am with you always, *even* to the end of the age."

The contest winners were Jubilee Worship Center in Hobart, Indiana, and Step by Step Ministries in Porter, Indiana. You can read their stories and learn amazingly effective ways to help unsaved people choose to accept Salvation in *Witnessing Made Easy: Yes, You Can Make a Difference* (Jubilee Worship Center Step by Step Press, 2010) by Bishop Dale P. Combs, Lisa Combs, Jim Barbarossa, Carla Barbarossa, and me. Six of the many other worthy ideas and practices from the contest for leading more people to learn about and some to be moved by the Holy Spirit to pledge their lives to Jesus are described in a second book, *Ways You Can Witness: How the Lost Are Found* (Salvation Press, 2010) by Cherie Hill, Roger de Brabant, Drew Dickens, Gael Torcise, Wendy Lobos, Herpha Jane Obod, Gisele Umugiraneza, and me.

Let me tell you another interesting thing about my life with Jesus. When my daughter was about a year old, I suffered what resembled a stroke that caused me to start to become paralyzed. As I could feel my face's muscles freezing, I immediately prayed to Jesus to stop the paralysis and He did. I was left with a lot of pain and numbness on the left side of my body and was very weak for over a year.

Part of that pain continued for the next twenty-two years until, on November 8, 2009, I asked two of my pastors during a communion service to pray in the name of Jesus that the remaining pain be removed. During the prayer, the pain started leaving immediately and was totally gone within a half hour. As I felt the pain leaving me, through some power traveling inch by inch down my body, I was overcome with gratitude and fell on my knees in thanks.

That wasn't the only time He recently healed me. Encouraged by that miraculous experience, I came forward again on December 19, 2010, during another communion service to request prayer for relief from the pain in my wrists that was making it difficult for me to write books to serve Him and to do my other work. Knowing that my mother had been plagued with arthritis, I assumed it was a similar onset for me. My pastors were occupied with prayers for other members of the congregation. This time an elder of the church and his wife anointed me with oil and prayed for me. Almost immediately, my whole body shook violently in a way that I couldn't stop. Gradually, the shaking was reduced until it stopped after about half an hour, and my wrist pain was totally gone. It has not returned. I was even more overwhelmed that He had healed me again. Can anyone appreciate all the goodness that God has in store for us?

Let me share yet another miraculous healing (not the last that I've experienced). I've always been troubled with many respiratory and food allergies and sensitivities. In my sixties, these problems had grown worse. I finally reached the point where it was difficult to be in the same room with other people, due to my reactions to any deodorants and scents they were using. During still another communion service on January 16, 2012, two pastors again prayed for me to be relieved of these problems so that I could be a better witness for Him. Once again, power filled my body. My allergies and sensitivities were gone in a few minutes. Since then, they haven't returned. Receiving this grace has made a huge improvement in my life and in my witnessing.

I have also been saved by God from what I believed to be certain death on twelve occasions, most recently on July 2, 2013. I won't go into all of these events, but I did want you to be aware that He is always touching all aspects of my life in beneficial ways.

While it's up to God to decide if and when He wants to heal us or to protect us from harm, it's certainly reassuring to know that He has the ability and power to do anything He wants.

Glory be to God! Praise Him always! His miracles, grace, and mercy never end. I am so happy and honored to be His servant and witness to you.

www.ingramcontent.com/pod-product-compliance
Lightning Source LLC
Chambersburg PA
CBHW060321200326
41519CB00011BA/1794